# STORYSCAPING

## STOP CREATING ADS, START CREATING WORLDS

Gaston Legorburu & Darren McColl
*SapientNitro*

**WILEY**

Cover image and design: John Starr, SapientNitro
Illustrations: Ariel Bellumio, Jorge Viera, Andrew Lopez, Rafael Jimenez, SapientNitro
Infographics: Francis Ferrazza, SapientNitro
Photography: Antonio Caballero, SapientNitro

This book is printed on acid-free paper.

Published by John Wiley & Sons, Inc., Hoboken, New Jersey.

Published simultaneously in Canada.

For general information about our other products and services, please contact our Customer Care Department within the United States at (800) 762-2974, outside the United States at (317) 572-3993 or fax (317) 572-4002.

Wiley publishes in a variety of print and electronic formats and by print-on-demand. Some material included with standard print versions of this book may not be included in e-books or in print-on-demand. If this book refers to media such as a CD or DVD that is not included in the version you purchased, you may download this material at http://booksupport.wiley.com. For more information about Wiley products, visit www.wiley.com.

ISBN 978-1-118-82328-6 (cloth); ISBN 978-1-118-87134-8 (ebk); ISBN 978-1-118-87123-2 (ebk)

Printed in the United States of America

10  9  8  7  6  5  4  3  2

# CONTENTS

# PART TWO

**77**

*Storyscaping Immersive Experiences for Powerful Brand and Consumer Connections*

# ACKNOWLEDGMENTS

The truth is, although we gave birth to the term *Storyscaping* during a client conference, the whole concept had been forming in our halls for years. This was hardly a bolt from the blue. In no way do we claim to be the sole architects of this thinking. What we did was play the role of curator, connector, and craftsperson. Credit goes to Laura McFarlane, who had been working for years on the concept of the "experience space"; Dr. Todd Cherkasky, Dr. Rick Robinson, and John Cain, who taught us all the power of ethnography; Sheldon Monteiro, who showed us how to leverage technology in order to enable amazing experiences; Donald Chesnut, for insight into the world of experience design and innovation; and the entire and wonderful team at SapientNitro, who have helped challenge, test, and evolve the perspective and practices in so many ways and on so many levels. Also, to our clients, who inspire us to challenge convention and change the game every day. And, of course, to Malcolm Poynton, who had been preaching to all of us to stop using a period and the end of every TV spot and start using the all-mighty comma.

Special thanks goes to Alan Herrick, Bill Kanarick, and the rest of our leadership team, who encouraged us to write this thing in the first place and to our passionate and brilliant team, without whom this book would have been nothing but an idea: Kiran, for project managing absolutely everything; Liz, for your calm and inspiring team management; John, Ariel, Jorge, Andrew, Rafael, and Francis for our fantastic cover, images, and design work; Sarah, for her words of wit and wonder; Sopurkha, for her editorial wizardry and spiritual balance; and Michelle and Dana, for managing our world and ensuring we had time to write.

And finally, to our loved ones, Amanda, Elizabeth, Michelle, and Little G, who have provided unwavering support and understanding throughout.

# ABOUT THE AUTHORS

## Gaston Legorburu
*Worldwide Chief Creative Officer*

Gaston Legorburu sets the strategic and creative vision for SapientNitro and its integrated marketing, brand communications, and commerce services. He has a passion for redefining how brands and consumers connect. This key focus has been instrumental in expanding SapientNitro's success beyond its deep digital roots. Today the agency is breaking traditional barriers and has evolved to become a trusted brand steward for some of the world's top brands.

Recognized by *Adweek* and *Ad Age* as a game changer who is modeling the agency of the future, Legorburu is known for constantly challenging the advertising industry to evolve its thinking and its actions toward real connections that create experiences and build real relationships among real people.

Since cofounding Planning Group International (PGI) in 1992—now the core of Sapient's Miami presence—Sapient turned industry heads when it became the first interactive agency to acquire an above-the-line shop, Nitro Group, and quickly gained global acclaim with the award-winning "Best Job in the World" campaign.

Legorburu has been a driving force constantly working to evolve SapientNitro into a *new breed of storyteller for an always-on world*. Our unique Storyscaping approach and Idea Engineering framework mixes multidisciplinary teams of strategists, creatives, and technologists who reshape traditional brand storytelling into immersive experiences where consumers and brands truly connect.

During his tenure SapientNitro has grown into the largest worldwide independent agency and has racked up 14 Cannes Lions for its signature dish of "advertising as experiences."

Throughout his career, Legorburu has helped clients gain unparalleled insights into effectively marketing their products and services in today's increasingly complex marketplace. He continues to provide clients such as Citi, Coca-Cola, ESPN, Chrysler, and Unilever, among others, with innovative solutions to critical business challenges.

Widely recognized as a thought leader, Legorburu is frequently quoted in publications such as *Advertising Age, Adweek, Bloomberg, Fast Company,* and the *Wall Street Journal* and is a member of TED. He sits on the 4A's digital board and the ADC advisory team. He is a sought-after speaker who has presented at notable industry conferences including Cannes Lions International Festival of Creativity, SXSW, ad:tech, OMMA Global, and SHOOT.

Legorburu is the recipient of numerous awards across the creative and advertising industry and has served as a judge for several prestigious award shows, including D&AD, Cannes Lions International Festival of Creativity, Art Directors Club, and the Webbys. He is also an active member of the Webby's International Academy of Digital Arts and Sciences.

If there were truly an office in the sky, that's probably where you'd find Legorburu, or you might catch him in SapientNitro's Miami office. His fun side reveals a Harley-Davidson riding, open-ocean fishing, artistic painter who enjoys life and making people laugh.

## Darren (Daz) McColl, BA, FAMI, CPM
### *Chief Brand Strategy Officer, Global*

As a Vice President and Chief Brand Strategy Officer for SapientNitro, Darren McColl's primary role is to help business grow by bringing insight to strategy and inspiration to creativity. He's passionate about new ideas and almost obsessive with the psychology of why people do things.

Big in life and in presence, McColl joined SapientNitro in 2009. He has guided the shape of marketing strategy since joining Gaston Legorburu and the team in the United States. Always testing new approaches and thinking in the cauldron of real client work, he is as practical a strategist as you could find.

His common sense and business focus is built from more than two decades of marketing toil in both client and agency roles. This hybrid and well-aged perspective gives him an advantage when mapping out branding and marketing strategies. He has imparted this wisdom to numerous global brands, such as Virgin Blue Airlines, Virgin Megastore, McDonald's, Nestlé, Mars, Foster's Lager, Burger King, Subway, Foot Locker, Coca-Cola Brands, X Games & ESPN, Chrysler, Mercedes-Benz, Volvo, Visit Florida, and Grupo BBVA. His most recognized and award-winning accomplishment was earned for spearheading the strategy behind the "Best Job in the World" campaign for Tourism and Events Queensland.

McColl has been internationally recognized as one of the world's leading strategists, with work awarded by three Cannes Lion Grands Prix, multiple Effies, MIXX Awards, New York Festivals, One Show, CLIOs, and D&D. Additionally, his expert thought leadership has appeared in notable trade publications and marketing textbooks.

He is a regular speaker at events and conferences around the world, from the Cannes Lions International Festival of Creativity to SXSW, Social Media Week, 4AAA's events, tourism conferences, and the like. He has served as a judge for awards in marketing, advertising effectiveness, strategy, and creativity.

A Fellow of the Australian Marketing Institute, McColl holds a BA from RMIT University.

Although a well-seasoned international business traveler, Miami is his base where he lives with wife, Amanda, and two Australian-born miniature schnauzers, Maverick and Elle.

# PART ONE

*Great Storytelling Alone Won't Save Your Business*

# INTRODUCTION

Every great story starts somewhere. This one has been brewing in our hallways for many years and officially grew wings early in 2012.

A client, one of the world's largest consumer packaged goods brands, hosted an event in London titled "Storytelling in the Digital Age." The company's chief marketing officer (CMO), was driving this initiative, supported by his group of lieutenants; all of the heads of the brands and the marketing directors from around the world were present. The CMO, arguably one of the most influential marketers in the world at the time, had recently declared that he would mandate a much larger percentage of the corporation's sizable global marketing spend to digital. His team put together this symposium as a way to get their heads wrapped around how to take their marketing approach into the digital space. Their request from partners like us was simple: Give them two to three things they could go to work on, starting the following week; give them something they could actually change. They wanted very actionable stuff and not a lot of it. At the event, presenters included their four global digital agencies, SapientNitro being one. Of course, all the usual suspects, such as Twitter, Google, and Facebook, were prominently represented. Additionally, they had their public relations (PR) agencies present, which was brilliant, as the world of PR has probably seen more disruption from the hyper-connected world than any other. PR is also going through some real struggles in terms of reinventing themselves—today a press release alone just doesn't work. Everything in that world has shifted dramatically to social, and many PR agencies are no longer effective because they haven't evolved, while others are encroaching into the digital marketing space with some success.

Picture the room with these players in their corners. There is clearly something interesting happening with PR agencies, clearly explosive growth with Google, Facebook, and Twitter in the digital social media space, and then there's something transformative going on in the digital agency space as well, right? In our view, we're all fighting for control of the same damn idea. These guys wanted to tap into that collective, to learn how to evolve its approach to building brands. Each of these representatives, in their respective corners, all attended this event in London to present their perspective on how this global organization could most effectively take advantage of this new space and adapt to quickly tackle any challenges that could be in their way of doing this.

Malcolm Poynton, our creative lead in Europe, was originally scheduled to speak on SapientNitro's behalf. At the last minute, Malcolm was called to a big pitch. He knew I happened to be in London, so he asked me to step in for him. "Sure, I'll do it," I said. "Where's your presentation?" That's when he gave me a time-stopping, blank stare. I realized we needed to roll up our shirtsleeves and put a killer presentation together. And we did just that. Enter: The language of Storyscaping.

While addressing this audience for whom we have a lot of respect, we knew that approaching them with a philosophy about how everything they once knew is now *all wrong* wouldn't feel right or go over well. First, it's pretty obnoxious, and second, it's not true. We believe that what this industry has been doing is overstating this conflict between new and old. There are things we have known, and there are things we now know. We encouraged this audience to recognize that there isn't some black and white line you cross from being traditional to going digital. If you're very rooted in the craft of advertising, as in the *Mad Men* era, and you haven't evolved, frankly, you might be a little screwed. And if you came from that era, crossed over the line, and forgot everything you once knew, well, then you also might be a little screwed. Or, if you think that the world started yesterday and only what happens tomorrow matters, then, you guessed it, still screwed. Isn't it a relief to hear that this period in marketing history doesn't require a total revolution? To dismiss thousands of years of storytelling and a hundred years of advertising and the psychology behind it would be an unhealthy loss. It's time to evolve it. Evolve your craft from one of using pictures and words into one of creating an immersive experience that encourages people to jump in and participate with your brand and become part of a shared story, not just your world *but their world*. Think of it as moving from using the 8-crayon box to the 24-crayon box. It's really that simple.

Our approach with these marketers was, "We value what you value in the power of story and building brands and making emotional connections." Our process with them was the same one we share with you here. First, we deconstructed what we all knew about stories, ads, and history. Then we added, rather than replaced, the new stuff we'd learned about storytelling in the digital era. After those two important steps were discussed and collaborated upon, then and only then could we connect the dots by applying Systems Thinking. Last, we leveraged new technology to build effective Story Systems. This is the essential formula for how we create immersive experiences where brands become part of people's stories and people become part of the brand's story.

At the conclusion of our keynote presentation, one of those semimagical moments that surface only when one deeply connects to the audience materialized. After stating, "We should all move from storytelling to Storyscaping," everyone in the room dropped their heads and pushed pens across paper for the first time during the event. It was that momentary dream state where we all collectively realized this language and approach enable a new way of connecting to this material. We put a name and a face on something they already envisioned but could not articulate or touch. Now they could more easily maneuver and attack this incredible opportunity created by this changing landscape in a very practical way.

Are you wondering how the story of our little presentation ended? Well, the good news is that it hasn't ended; it continues to evolve. Soon after that fateful day, we were approached and asked to present this concept during many industry events, including the sixtieth annual Cannes Lions International Festival of Creativity, and most notably to many senior business leaders and marketing professionals around the world. The funny, yet reassuring bit is that many of those folks (whom we are proud to call clients) have not only adopted this language and philosophy but made it theirs. It's fun when we find ourselves in conversations where they "critique" whether something we are proposing is appropriate for their *Storyscape* or aligns to their *Organizing Idea*. We are thrilled by the fact that they now own this idea. When a concept is lifted by those kinds of wings and boomerangs back, it's probably time to write the book on it.

Speaking of books, perhaps you've noticed the plethora of new business books that tout the power of storytelling being published these days. In case you had not already tuned in, the majority of those books will convince you that story is a powerful elixir that can magically connect your business to new customers in a meaningful and profitable way. They will also prove beyond a reasonable doubt that the best-run companies and the most successful brands all have a great story to tell. We believe that to be *mostly true*, but what those books fail to point out is that not just any old story will do the trick. You need a great story, one with much more than just words and pictures. You need to create immersive worlds. Create worlds that resonate with the highly connected, digitally enabled consumer of today. Create sensing and adaptive worlds that, in this ever-changing environment, can differentiate and cut across emotional, physical, and virtual experiences. Whether you are an entrepreneur just getting started, part of a world-class team, or sitting in the big chair, in a big office, at a big company, this book aims to help you better understand and imagine these immersive experiences. It will also show you how to combine storytelling with Systems Thinking, becoming a valuable guide on how to leverage enabling technologies in order to create powerful Story Systems. Maybe you're feeling frustrated that your marketing efforts are failing to keep up and your company is on the verge of disappearing, or perhaps things are working well but your ambitions always trump your achievements and you want to take things to the next level. Either way, this book can unlock some real opportunity for you and your organization. Don't just throw more spaghetti at the wall to see what sticks or repackage and repurpose all the same stuff you've been using and watch it underthrill again. You can now stop telling the world your story though ads alone and learn how to create worlds in which your stories become part of the consumers' world. This is why we warm-heartedly encourage you to stop story-yelling and start Storyscaping—or *stop creating ads and start creating worlds.*

**The Fast, Cheap, and Good Rule.** We are not sure who came up with this old notion, but we think the first time we heard it was from a building contractor during our office remodel. "Pick two," he requested. "You can have your office done *fast* and *good,* but it won't be *cheap.* Or, we can do it *fast* and *cheap,* but it won't be *good.*" He reinforced his delivery on any combination of those two elements with a caveat: We should expect to sacrifice on the third element. We think the opposite exists in any market-facing business. Here we use the same idea of juggling three relatable components in a formula, only this time we plug in **value, story,** and **experience.** Unlike the previous "rule" where two elements were reductive to the third, this logic amplifies the third. For example, if you provide great *value* and create a great *experience,* you will improve your *story.* If you have a great *story* and you provide a great *experience,* you amplify your *value.* We will explore the relationship between experience and product further in this book because we believe they are interchangeable ideas—or at least highly related. The same goes for value and price. If you provide a great experience (product) and have a great story (brand), you should be able to merit higher value (price). It's time to recognize that any fool can offer a discount to sell more product or service, printing a bunch of coupons or promoting buy-one-get-one-free offers or even renting a chicken suit—these options do not take much imagination and are rather shortsighted. On the flip side, savvy marketers can differentiate their product or service by crafting a memorable brand story that emotionally connects a company to its customers through shared values. This option requires real imagination and some emotional intelligence. Trumping all of these options is the genius who puts it all together by connecting a great story with an immersive and differentiated experience at the right price. With that said, another great way to differentiate and grow is to re-imagine how a product or service is delivered by creating new business models, a truly differentiated experience, or innovation. It takes a visionary to pull that off. How do you differentiate and grow your business?

The following is a taste of what we are concocting throughout this book—a snapshot of four main approaches to marketing. First we offer a hypothetical example about a pizza store, designed as a useful, quick look at how your any-size, any-type business compares within a simplified framework. Next, using that same framework, we provide highly recognizable real-world examples to further drive home our points.

**Price-Based Differentiation.** *Sue Generic owns a pizza delivery company. There are two similar pizza joints in her small town. In order to grow her business, Sue chooses to advertise her pizza with a buy-one-get-one-free offer.* In our view, Sue is not telling a good story. In fact, you could argue that the story could be interpreted as, "This is cheap pizza." Now, of course, she has the best intentions; after all, doesn't everyone want a good deal? The short answer is, discounting alone is almost always a bad idea in the long run. Price-based differentiation can often be a one-way ticket to commoditization, not to mention abysmal margins.

**Story-Based Differentiation.** *Sue Generic owns a pizza delivery company. There are two pizza joints in her small town, but hers is different. In order to* *differentiate her business, Sue shares her story with her customers and the public in clever and relevant ways. Sue tells how she learned to make their secret sauce when she was only 12. Sue uses the recipe that has been in her family for 100 years, and she imports all the key ingredients weekly, including the "secret" herbs for the sauce. New customers line up to try her family recipe every day. She never takes reservations, never rushes an order, and closes early when she runs out of pie dough for the day.*

**Experience-Based Differentiation.** *Sue Generic owns a pizza delivery company. There are two other similar pizza joints in her small town, but she intends to change the game. In order to grow her business, Sue chooses to offer guaranteed delivery in 30 minutes or less. She has even invested in a mobile app that allows her very busy customers to order their favorite custom pie on the fly so they can get those kids fed and in bed tonight. Hers is the only pizza joint to offer this differentiated experience, and her customer base keeps growing.*

**Storyscaping Differentiation.** *Sue Generic owns a pizza delivery company. There are two other pizza joints in her small town, but they cannot compete with hers. Sue understands that to build a successful business she must do all of the above while carefully balancing elements of **value, story,** and **experience** with a sharp focus on becoming part of her customers' world. She reimagined the whole business, she has a story that truly connects with people, and she created an experience that delivers a product that can't easily be replicated, for which her customers happily pay a premium. Sue is a genius!*

Now that you have a generic glimpse of the four main approaches and how they work within their respective frameworks, the following real-world examples from the toy industry aim to add more practical fuel for comprehension.

**Price-Based Differentiation.** We don't want to give this idea too much airtime, nor does it really merit any further explanation. You can find plenty of this crap all around you. The world does not need yet another factory in China making nameless blue teddy bears. We will use blue teddy bears as our example of price-based differentiation. They are $7.99, and that's about all they have going for them. They could be handy if you find yourself in a situation where you need to buy a gift for a kid you don't know well or like much . . . and they are blue . . . don't you want one?

**Story-Based Differentiation.** Of course you remember the famous Cabbage Patch Kids of the early 1980s, right? *Materially speaking, Cabbage Patch Kids were not too different from other dolls on the shelf next to it. They did not have computer chips in them, they did not move, they didn't talk, they didn't create sounds or flash any lights—on no account were they better than any other doll. What stood out was their unique element of story; each Cabbage Patch Kid had to be "adopted," which made the whole story as much (or more) about the buyer as it did the product.[1] This is why people paid toy retailers and other outlets premium prices and paid doll scalpers and collectors four times those premium prices for a Cabbage Patch Kid as they would have paid for a similar doll.[2] Today an original Cabbage Patch Kid will still fetch a handsome price on eBay. The key here is that their story put you, the "adoptive parent," in the middle.* This is exactly the kind of story we will introduce and encourage throughout the pages of this book. It's not easy to craft the right story, but when you do, the effects are vast, powerful, and long lasting.

**Experience-Based Differentiation.** Do you have a Build-a-Bear franchise store in your local mall? That store takes appointments. An appointment for a store that sells teddy bears? Why? *These guys have taken teddy bear sales to another level, and their success lies in the creation of immersive experiences.[3] Envision a magical place where you can take your favorite adolescent—be it your daughter, your nephew, or even yourself. When you arrive in this magical place, you embark on the journey of picking out just the right piece of soft fur, having it stuffed to your preferred 'squishiness' and giving it life with its very own heart (that you can kiss for good wishes before it's popped inside your new friend). After your bear is built to your liking, next you select the perfect outfit to take it home in. You can even add a sound and finally, the cherry on top of this customized magical experience, you get to give your new best friend a name.[4] Who could possibly deny their kid an experience like this, even at the hearty premium price it demands?* A differentiated experience like this one can grow your business fast, usually faster than a great brand story, but the trade-off is easy replication by your competitor. Therefore, the challenge with this approach is, and has always been, sustainability.

**Storyscaping Differentiation.** Let's explore the phenomenon of the American Girl franchise success. *In the 1980s, a publisher of educational materials came up with an idea to teach American History with the release of three 18-inch dolls, each from a different time period.[5] These dolls all came with historically accurate storybooks detailing their life. While the educational aspect of these dolls was their kick start, there was also much built-in entertainment from aftermarket sales of doll accessories and clothing. Around the time Mattel bought the company in 1995, there were more than 50 dolls, all with stories from all over the world in practically every ethnicity. Every little girl could finally identify on a physical level with a doll that mirrored* *her, that told her tale. Today, those young doll enthusiasts have a veritable American Girl universe of exquisite retail spaces to roam and collect dolls. They can dine in American Girl restaurants or get makeovers for themselves and their dolls at American Girl salons. Their Manhattan location is on 5th Avenue, a hotbed of frenzied birthday party waiting lists. You can browse the entire catalog on your iPad and download American Girl diary apps to your iPod. Doll owners heavily travel the social media space to share couture doll ensembles or to show off impressive collections of dolls that are on and off the market like antiques and artwork. There are real-life fashion shows of dolls and their owners. In 2012 American Girl reported millions of visitors annually, with sales at $100.5 million.[6] Their website gets more than 70 million hits per year.[7]* American Girl has a story with no periods, just commas. This is the kind of Storyscape we will delve into throughout this book—and after examining the differences between these four approaches, we think you'll agree: Storyscaping is a methodology well worth delving into, and there is fun to be had along the way.

Let's remain positive during the challenges we are all facing in the market today and evolve our craft. Look at this time as an opportunity to re-imagine your business. What will happen when you start focusing on creating a *world* around your business? How much more effective do you think your efforts will be when your *world* personally affects each individual consumer's story? What if every interaction that occurred between a consumer and your business led to immersive experiences, making your customers want to jump into your *world* and become part of your narrative? Conversely, if you get to be in their story, then by nature, don't they too become part of your story? Imagine how creating *shared stories* could make an awfully big impact on consumer engagement and brand advocacy. This scene displays what we call the leap from storytelling (creating ads) into Storyscaping (creating worlds). This is a pretty powerful leap. It is revolutionary and evolutionary, and with it, our aim is to make marketing in the digital age more accessible for everyone. To do that, we are about to share with you our approach and full model for bringing it all together while we highlight real-client work. You'll see it's actually rather simple, and when you get into a groove with it, it makes your work enjoyable.

In Part One you'll gain an essential foundational understanding of the purpose and power behind Storyscaping; you will also connect with some real-world examples through case studies and enjoy supporting interviews from some of the most influential marketing leaders. Part Two is where we share details behind the how-to, giving you a step-by-step model that you can use to shift your efforts today toward affecting successful evolution for your organization and brand in the near future. Through this book, SapientNitro has taken a major step toward increased transparency, proving our willingness to share our approach with the entire industry. We wrote this in a style and language that is intended for an audience of the solo, self-employed businessperson working to make a difference on a local level, on up through the multiteam departments of worldwide brands. We also hope this helps our "competitors" who know firsthand how tough it is to consistently evolve—each of us aspiring to be the best in a new breed of storytellers. We share our successful approach here with everyone who is willing to evolve their business and brand. We offer our transperency to those who are willing to try something a little new, to make positive advancements on several key levels within their own organizations. Storyscaping is how you transform a great story line into an immersive Story System where people enjoy their connection

with your brand and want to continue their loyalty and be a coparticipant in your *world*. May this concept and step-by-step model put you back in the marketing driver's seat and fill your company with deeper connections to the people you care about as they invite your brand to be a part of their worlds. Happy Storyscaping!

# FROM THE CAMPFIRE

*Making Sense of the World through Story*

# FROM THE CAMPFIRE

*Making Sense of the World through Story*

Humans have an innate ability to take disparate events and connect them together to create meaning. This is how we understand the workings and threads of the world. A quick peek into prehistoric archaeology reveals that this is how we've pretty much always done it. In 2012, a team of archaeologists from the University of Bristol studied 11 subterranean caves located along Spain's Cantabrian Coast. In one of those caves, El Castillo,[1] they discovered the remains of the earliest-known cave paintings.[2] They are a million years old. An unrelated archaeological discovery, this one in Wonderwerk Cave in South Africa, has recently unearthed findings of the earliest solid evidence that our ancient human forebears were using fire. That's right, the first known campfire, which also dates back to a million years ago. From these discoveries, it is surmised that cavemen and cavewomen gathered together seeking to share experiences and to narrate and record their stories as much as they gathered for the physical warmth of the campfire.

Today, the early origins of those campfire scenes are often used as the obvious illustration of the history and communal value of storytelling. Although that illustration may be helpful, we believe the caveman himself and the origin of language is the more appropriate example to illustrate the value we humans get from stories. Envision a world before structured language, where grunts, frowns, and actions that included a hell of a lot of pointing and hand gestures did all the communicating. We can make the guess that back then literally showing someone something was the very best way of explaining it. Please park that concept in your head for now, and we will show you how actions and experiences are also important elements of communication. Before structured language, it was very difficult to express complex thoughts. Even today, it is challenging to string together multiple ideas or even simple concepts without a system or pattern. We use stories as a figurative glue that solidifies a pattern and hardwires it into our brain. Stories are our way of making sense of the world. We relate to places, events, people, objects, and ideas through stories. Religions are powered by stories, wars break out because of stories, and your children are shaped through stories. Just try to make sense of a series of events, or describe something monumental that happened in history, or simply tell us about yourself without leveraging a story. It's difficult. Stories help us understand and organize just about everything. Why is your favorite place your favorite place? Chances are because there's a story there. Or what about how your favorite room in an old family house makes you feel transported. Why does that happen? It's probably because of the pictures in your mind, some might say, the storybook memories you created in that space. How do we choose our friends? Who attracts us? What connection do we make when something makes us feel good? The answer is story. Story is how we connect to place, to space, to people—always serving to help us make sense of the world. From million-year-old campfires to cave paintings to epic Greek odes, we've used story for a long time to make sense and sort through this existential miasma of meaning and survival.

**The Box with 8 Crayons.** Back to the basics to formulate a structured foundation. When creating anything, obviously, step 1 is to start somewhere. If you're a business owner just starting out and resources are minimal, stick with the basics and start by building a super-strong foundation from which you can grow and embellish. If you're a well-oiled marketing machine, it might still be a fun exercise to revisit the basics—for story, "the basics" = structure. Fortunately, all kinds of information on the structure of story has been researched and shared, and it's just a matter of getting familiar with what already exists and works for plotting a brand's story. We will briefly review some foundational aspects as seed for when you ramp up for Storyscaping. This is where strategy and Systems Thinking first come into play when creating an engaging story. Let's review this valuable groundwork.

We all know stories are structured. Stories have a plot, settings, characters, and narrative point of view. We often see these patterns even when they are not there. Have you ever intuitively predicted what would happen next in a book or a movie? In storytelling, structure is either something you deliberately design or something that unfolds organically, but it's always in there. Think of music with a verse, a chorus, and a bridge. Structure in this context does not mean creativity plays a backseat or that your work is formulaic. Think about these structures as building blocks for creativity. You design a structure to highlight the type of story you're telling. You have choices and creative license with your story and also with the determination of its structure. Structure is where you marry your craft with your art. Think of it as properly laying out the pieces of your model airplane before you glue it, paint it, and send it for flight.

British journalist and author Christopher Booker analyzed myths, folktales, literature, films, and a few soap operas for good measure. Seven hundred pages of his thorough study revealed some repeating patterns, patterns that distinguished seven basic plots,[3] which have been remastered over and over for all of story eternity. Do any of these sound familiar: overcoming the monster, rags to riches, the quest, voyage and return, rebirth, comedy, tragedy? Which plot is structuring your marketing today? Are you selling by way of *Beowulf, King Kong,* or *Aliens,* where you have a clearly identifiable evil, or "monster" who poses a threat to a group of people? Is your hero battling the monster, experiencing some losses over the course of action and then ultimately conquering and returning peace to the land? The fact is that some story structures, lend themselves more effectively for connecting brands and consumers and evoking real participation and social currency, similar to some musical structures, which lend themselves more to enticing people to dance. Some stories are more likely to get passed on from person to person and generation to generation. Joseph Campbell, the American mythologist, uncovered that very structure known as the hero's journey in his work.[4] Campbell suggests that, in this structure the audience connects to the hero through values such as community, justice, truth, and self-expression. We actually see ourselves as the hero in these stories. This formula is perfect for creating brand-consumer connections. Two contemporary examples of the hero's journey formula can be observed and explored in *The Wizard of Oz* and *Star Wars.* Both start with an unlikely hero, one who is ordinary and perhaps even helpless. Both Dorothy and Luke want to live out their higher values (they want justice in the world) but feel powerless to do anything about it. Then, through an interesting twist of events, they meet a mentor who gets them to realize that so much more is possible. The mentor gives them a magical gift—a pair of ruby red slippers or a lightsaber—and sends them off on a dangerous quest of self-discovery. During their adventures, which are filled with trials and tribulations, they both meet the source of brokenness in their world and they both seize a treasure or knowledge that they come back and utilize to heal society. Through this process, they ultimately learn much about themselves and the world in general. Now, imagine Dorothy or Luke as your customer and the mentor is your brand. Can you see how that could create bonds? The biggest mistake brands make in storytelling is to believe they must play the role of hero. This is just plain arrogant. Your product or service should play the role of those magical ruby slippers. TOMS Shoes is a great real-world brand example. TOMS is a company with a higher Purpose of "helping others in need."[5] Its business is simple; for every product you purchase, TOMS will help a person in need by donating a pair of shoes—you buy one; TOMS give one. The company started with shoes and quickly used this successful hero model to expand. TOMS is now also helping to restore sight by selling eyeglasses. The customer (the hero) and TOMS (the mentor) share a set of values, and the magic lies in the product (gift), which empowers customers to live their values by participating. Does your brand behave like a mentor? Does your company make or offer to give a gift?

Whether it's Neanderthal elbow rubbing or social media socializing, story is central to what it means to be human, and the best stories, the stories with mythic potential, all include a hero within their structure. Even the hero herself is structured: She needs to leave her normal life, face insurmountable obstacles, fall into the abyss of despair, receive supernatural intervention, and eventually return with some transformed aspect or trophy as proof of results of her transformative journey. Finding a way to make your customer the hero can be a scary place for many marketing professionals who were taught to make the brand the hero and the customer the target or "audience." You can empower your customers by making them the hero of your brand's narrative landscape. This is how you become part of their story—make your customer the hero and frankly, who better to tell your brand story than the hero herself?

**Step Up to the Big Box of 24 Crayons.** Beyond the basic structures, what's the next evolutionary leap for story? Well, there are certainly some exciting advances we can use to help bring story to the next level! Following the evolution of J. K. Rowling, the author of the Harry Potter series, from storyteller to Storyscaper serves as a supportive illustration. Although Rowling initially imagined the world of Harry Potter through a series of books (words and pictures), she has successfully taken Harry from the imaginary space to the physical and virtual space. In the world's eyes she is a great storyteller—in our eyes, she is also a great Storyscaper. To make the transformation, she didn't have to forget what she knew. Rather J. K. Rowling evolved by partnering with Thierry Coup, Sr. VP of Universal Creative to create the park experience, thereby expanding her palate to include space and environmental design, game design principles, application of sounds, smells, and a ton of creative technology.[6] She now colors with many more crayons, the way we all need to.

Our desires haven't changed much from universal story themes. But our methods of expressing a story have far advanced handprints, books, and movies for that matter. So why haven't all marketers or agencies kept up? Technology has made it possible for us to stretch the tool of "writing a story" into an ability to create immersive experiences and emotional engagements that are unprecedented. It's not hard. It just takes the right approach, the right model, and the right foundation. Nothing supersedes the human desire for meaningful experience. Our need to express our experience to others has simply migrated from cave drawings to tweets and posts. And they are still about the same experience of marking an existence, of expressing a human desire to connect with others via the camaraderie of experience. Taking a photo with your favorite pair of kicks is the most modern version of a cave painting from tens of thousands of years ago. It is the modern method of connecting with global citizens who also know what it is to love that same pair of sneakers. Keep in mind; most narrative is now interactive. Your customers have come a long way since scratching charcoal buffalos on cave walls as a way of expressing themselves. Marketers must refresh their approach; it's time to move from just creating universal stories to delivering ever-innovative ways of placing consumers at the center of these stories. The most successful marketing groups are reassigning consumers from the role of audience to the role of protagonist. It's their journey that matters.

Let's face it, everyone connects to story because in essence, we are story—we exist to see and to do and to be known. A story says simply, "I am here. See me." That's what is depicted and mythologized in the earliest forms of visual expression—campfire stories offered as cave paintings—the caveman's way of begging to not be forgotten.

You could say, when it comes to stories, there's just no telling. Oh, we still stand by the inherent value of a thousand-plus years of storytelling as one of the most important and impressionistic tools that we use as marketers to change perceptions and drive behaviors—that has *not* changed. Take what you've learned about story and move forward with it. Advertising needs to advance from just telling a story to affecting the experience or product. When you merely tell a story, you are not making a full connection. Evolve, engage the power of story, and now focus it around creating immersive experiences that you share with your consumers and that they'll want to share with their social circles. Enlist story as your currency for connection, and take it to a much more encompassing dimension: Elevate it using the power of experience. Remember, people are much more likely to remember and share their personal stories than they are to remember or spread yours.

**Story Is Our Currency.** We interviewed some brilliant people for this book to learn how other successful companies use story as currency. Coca-Cola's perspective proved particularly enlightening because of how steeped in story it has been for more than 125 years. Coca-Cola *is* story.[7] It is a brand more widely recognized and more widely distributed across the globe than any other. And story is as important to its business today as it has ever been.

Some companies have storytelling as a fundamental part of their heritage, and of course, some don't. Brands need a real Purpose and we often find that Purpose is connected to the great stories of the company. But today, the challenge extends through to how you leverage the power of stories and storytelling to propel your company.

At Coca-Cola, you can find one of the world's most valuable and most extensive branded archives. And for a deeper experience, there is the World of Coca-Cola in Atlanta. New employees start their careers at Coca-Cola by spending time immersed in the stories from the archives. Story, after story, after story reveals how the company was founded, how the company was built in America, how the company was built overseas, and how the company then started to build different brands. Storytelling is a genetic part of the company's DNA.

Not all companies stand for a set of "company" stories. Instead, the brands of the parent company have stories. When structured this way, it's a different challenge because the creative agenda resides in the brands, not the parent.

> *Understanding the relationship between core company stories and core brand stories has had a really dramatic effect on my belief on the power of storytelling. A powerful metaphor I often use when workshopping new ideas is one of the spider plant. If you can fill the central pot, i.e., the company, with great stories, then that will act as a fantastic fertilizer for all the baby plantlets, i.e., the brand stories that the mother plant will birth.*
>
> —Jonathan Mildenhall, Vice President of Global Advertising Strategy and Creative Excellence, The Coca-Cola Company

Within many stories, the Coca-Cola Company has a Purpose or ethos, or a defining story; a powerful platform that translates and filters down into the individual brands.

The company's overarching story and Purpose are very simple. "Coca-Cola is committed to *refreshing the world through moments of optimism and happiness, while creating value and making a difference wherever it goes.*" Coca-Cola's is a story of refreshment, happiness, optimism, and value. It's a strong and focused story, one that then flows into all of the brands. The folks who work with the brands ask questions such as, "Is this brand leaning into happiness? Is this brand leaning into optimism? Is this brand leaning into value? Is this brand leaning into refreshment? Or is this brand leaning into a cultural difference?" Asking these questions ensures that there isn't anything in the Coca-Cola Company that doesn't start from the company premise. In other words, the company won't do anything that doesn't refresh—no snack foods, no chips. Chips aren't refreshing, but juice and iced tea are. This is how the brand story follows the organizing discipline set by the parent company and then flows across the entire company. If it doesn't refresh by creating value through optimism and happiness, it's not being made by the Coca-Cola Company.

Today's consumer looks at a company's ethos and holds it and its brands to that ethos. This is especially the case now with the expectation and reality of transparency—we have to face facts; people know us beyond what we are saying in our marketing. They know exactly what we're all doing, how we treat employees, where we get our supplies, along with everything else. So it's more important to make sure you're focused not solely on how you communicate the story but also on the way that you behave. Take a moment and assess how well you and your company are addressing the challenge of behaving true to your Purpose.

As an example, look at the now long-standing cultural trend that is leaning toward a theme of environmental care. People want to be greener—or be seen as being greener—and they want to leave the world better than how they found it. Have you noticed the many companies that now position their products or services around that idea? Have you questioned whether or not they're actually behaving that way? Some of them don't align their behavior. And people notice and then vote with their wallets. Your stories and behaviors need to be aligned and aligned not just with each other but with consumer perception and expectations. Don't be like an oil company that talks about what it's doing to save the rain forest; it's hypocritical. Work toward gaining a common connection in business behavior, consumer expectation, and Brand Purpose.

**Double This and Half That.** When a big company plans to double the size of production, the shareholders are feeling great and seeing dollar signs while the environmentalists get that sinking feeling in their stomachs. Unilever recognized this imbalance. So when Unilever came out with a stated ambition to double the size of its business over the next 10 years, it coupled that with the ambition to also reduce its carbon footprint by 50 percent. One of the ways it's going to do that is by using biodegradable packaging for all of its products. Consider how much packaging and waste Unilever will eliminate across its entire supply chain—this is a significant effort that will make a positive difference, a real impact. The fact that Unilever immediately put measures in place to ensure a significant reduction of its carbon footprint can be viewed as a system-wide story and system-wide agenda-setting plan that satisfies all of its stakeholders.[8] And, it all starts with the power of a story on improved business.

We believe that really audacious leaders of companies should tell these bold stories to challenge our way of working, whether every chapter has been written yet or not. Such opportunities present possibility when you partner with the right people to fill in the pages.

We learned from James Cameron that sometimes you have to tell a story from the technology point forward, versus creating the story and waiting for technology to catch up. He thinks in both directions. Google is a bit like that. Google's Purpose is to organize the world's information.[9] Is there another company that can have as big of an ambition as what Google expresses? It truly takes a great story and technology. Google aims to achieve this worldwide organization by figuring out new ways to code things—how it works will potentially become a great story. And we say "potentially" because sometimes the technology exists but the wrong story is told about it. Presenting the story in a new way is sometimes how it catches on. Perhaps that was the case with Google+. The technology hasn't really shifted, but the first time Google told the story, it didn't catch on. But now, after revising the story, Google+ is enjoying solid growth. What is evident here is that you have to artfully connect both the story and the experience—that's key.

We all believe in and live out the power of story each day. That power is turbocharged when infused with the power of experience. And, they go hand in hand—the only way to share a personal experience that you've had in your life is to share it through a story. The dictionary definitions of *story* and *storytelling* describe a portrayal of a series of events and include experience as an element. Part of our thesis is that this experience element is incredibly powerful and often underleveraged. People are much more likely to remember stories that happened in their own lives than the ones that happen to others (or to brands). The more compelling a story is, the more likely people will connect with it or remember it. We encourage you to ask yourself some pointed questions: How do I, as a marketer, think about the experience element? Is my brand forming an emotional connection? Does my brand, product, or service become part of my consumer's story?

**Talk About Ripple Effect.** Rarely does a marketing effort start with an experience. Most often, the expectation is to communicate a message.

The way most agencies work is from a storytelling perspective versus a story-experiencing perspective. When you aim for experiential storytelling, it's easier to turn that into exponential storytelling. The creation of an experience for 100 people and then the subsequent online viewing of that experience by a million people is a highly accessible possibility to just about anyone. This is an increasing trend known as splashes and ripples, and it should be leveraged more. But when you're looking at your media plan, it's not from this perspective. Today it could be the splash of an event and the ripple of the response, the content, the reviews, and so on. Looking at the metrics of experiential event marketing doesn't give us the return or impact of the ripples. Therefore, when trying to optimize your marketing investments, remember that there's a shifting of value across those things; don't think solely about what it costs to generate that splash without accounting for the value of those ripples.

We challenge you to look to create a splash for great content and then amplify that content around the world. Some splashes live in real-time dialogue for years after the event is over. Nike created a 3-minute production for $20 million to generate splash on YouTube and its Facebook for two days. By all media measures it was not just a splash; it was an atomic bomb that immediately stirred up world sentiment about the World Cup—and Nike wasn't even an official sponsor. Then there was ongoing dialogue that rippled everywhere because Nike inspired you to be part of it.[10] It extended the conversation and ripples right through the tournament.

There is more power in starting your story from a little concept that we call the Organizing Idea, an idea that is an active expression meant to inspire experiences, not a brand statement.

A great example is Coca-Cola's "Open Happiness." This is an active expression that can drive participation and experience. It connects with people, and these people become part of the story or contribute to it.

Let's do a simple brand marketing comparison to get you thinking about the point we are making here. Take Pepsi's "Taste of a New Generation" and Coke's "Open Happiness." Think about each expression. Where could you take the marketing for each? Does one seem more actionable than the other? Is one easier to relate to, connect to, and engage with?

Coca-Cola's "Open Happiness" marketing platform is more than storytelling; it is storydoing. This is because if you're going to "open" happiness, you have to actually do something.

*"Increasingly, consumers expect brands to do more than what is just suggested by the category they're in. They certainly expect Coca-Cola to do more than just refresh them from an intrinsic point of view. Our commitment to local community programs reflects this. We are champions of female equality and run extensive female entrepreneur initiatives. We proudly distribute HIV and AIDS medicine across Africa. We invest in creating fresh drinking water for kids in the different jungles of Brazil. Teens and mums alike are like, "Yes, we're going to buy your beverages, but you better be doing lots of things in my local community to make my local community better!"*

*"I think that's a mandate for a lot of brands to move from storytelling, however rigorous or inspirational that storytelling is, to actual storydoing, as there is a growing need for brands to occupy positive spaces in different communities around the world."*
—Jonathan Mildenhall, Vice President of Global Advertising Strategy and Creative Excellence, The Coca-Cola Company

# YOUR FIRST KISS

*Harnessing the Power of Experience*

# YOUR FIRST KISS

*Harnessing the Power of Experience*

Every brand needs a story. If the role of story is the most powerful tool for connecting brands to consumers, is it possible to evolve that connection into a relationship? Yes! Meet the power of experience; it catapults the effects of storytelling. It is the element within the definition of storytelling that we believe is the most powerful, yet in most stories, remains sorely underleveraged: *Storytelling: Sharing of events with words, images, sounds and/or experiences, sometimes with improvisation or embellishment.* Experiences are more powerful than pictures and words alone. The best stories are ones that also create shared experiences. People don't just want to be told a story; they want to be part of the story. In the past, the way we had become accustomed to marketing our businesses was more about the telling, primarily using words and images. And that worked pretty darn well for about 100 years. We still use those elements, and now with the onslaught of technology advances, we can evolve *telling* into shared experiences between the consumer and the brand. What is so important about this thing we keep calling experience? It has to do with creating deeper connections, increasing retention, and extending loyalty.

**Power of Experience.** We remember and retain stories about ourselves much more vividly than we remember stories about others, because we've *experienced* them. Think back on your first kiss. Now think about how reading a really well-written story about someone's first kiss can facilitate a connection in your mind to your own first kiss, thereby connecting you to the story. How about watching an amazing film about somebody's first kiss—a film with great acting, great directing, and great camera work—see how that not only makes the connection but takes to the next level? What about when you hear a secondhand story about a friend's first kiss? This also makes a connection, partly because it's someone you know, partly because that personal reference probably makes the story rather entertaining and perhaps the connection here is even deeper because of our natural instinct to compare. But your own first kiss? The experience of your own first kiss . . . you can still feel it now, can't you? It's unlike reading, watching, or hearing about anyone else's first kiss—because *you experienced it*. If you had never experienced your own first kiss, the connections you made to the stories of other people's first kiss would not be nearly as strong. This is why experience should be the element that marketing plans and maybe even business models are designed with. We must all look for ways to create opportunities for consumers to have "first kisses" with our brands, rather than just telling them about our brand. This is story making versus storytelling; there's a big difference. Start designing your marketing efforts toward offering first kiss experiences—in several ways and in several areas simultaneously if you can. Facilitate opportunities for your consumers to have experiences with you wherever and whenever they want.

A first kiss is memorable. A first kiss is emotional. A first kiss hardwires itself in the brain. A first kiss can be reexperienced with every new partner. Each time we lean in toward the next new set of lips, our anticipation engages all the senses until they stand on end. This is the emotional and physical response you are looking to create for each experience with your brand. Then human nature kicks in and our minds replay all these first kiss experiences. If you've lived on the edge a bit, maybe you had a first kiss with someone of a different race or religion. You replay it. How about lip-locking with someone of the same sex? You replay it. Extramarital affair first kiss? You replay it. Or, more seriously, that moment in the birthing room of the hospital with your newborn, your first kiss with this new life . . . you replay it. Create experiences with your brand that people want to replay, like they do their first kiss. Create experiences that make people want to come back again and again and reexperience your brand in a variety of ways. In other words, as a brand, create more experiences to increase brand retention. The more you reengage consumers, the more they remember you and stick with you, thereby extending their brand connection. You have to keep kissing!

Experience is also a powerful platform for learning and building knowledge. When you were two years old, your mom undoubtedly told you 50 times not to touch the hot stove. Inevitably, you did. In that moment, you not only burned your skin but burned and branded an experience into your brain, which became part of your story. That experience sits more deeply grounded in your mind than your mom's audio loop. In the story of "don't touch the hot stove," your mom = storyteller and you = story maker. Why? Because you experienced it. It becomes knowledge for future reference and telling, and possibly even leaves a little scar.

People will much more vividly retain an experience of actually traveling to Nepal or to Sao Paulo or to Brooklyn for the first time than they would if they read a book about any of these destinations, right? And, not only are people more likely to remember personal experiences, they are much more likely to share the memories of those experiences with other people, possibly influencing them to try the experience, too. Experience engenders further storytelling. With the amplification of technology, an experience can be so much more than a splash; it can send ripples everywhere.

What is it that brought us to this point of having to evolve our storytelling into Storyscaping? Let's examine some of the changes that are driving this necessity.

**Consumer Expectations.** One of the biggest challenges is that consumer expectations are off the dial. They are extreme both in the speed with which they shift and also the fact that they set new norms on a constant basis. Consumers are also inspired to review, critique, assess, and analyze everything from socks to political parties. There is a newfound relationship with content, and with it, a social pressure to be involved by sharing it. This has given consumers a new world of power and influence.

Today's consumers have totally forgotten how we used to walk to find a payphone to make a call—on a rotary dial. We needed a quarter to start and fumbled for more change when the conversation went on longer than 3 minutes. They are unaware of the concept of having to wait to make a phone call. Modern consumers have phones that pay their bills, locate their children, make videos, map out car trips, and even tell them what to cook for dinner, in any language. We get all this with the press, click, and swipe of a screen or two. What's more, you can do any of these, and about 3 billion other things, electronically 24 / 7 / 365. As a society, we have so quickly adapted to this convenience that it has become a full-on expectation, and when something, a-n-y-thing happens to disrupt this flow of fingertip availability, beware; the whole world is going to know about it . . . as soon as the whole world is back up and running that is (which, to our point, will most likely just be in just a matter of moments).

Posts, status updates, live streaming videos, and tweets are some ways of hearing a fellow consumer's opinion about any service, product, brand, or respective representative he or she interacts with throughout any given day or night. This creates a living, dynamic "rap sheet" or trophy shelf, whichever applies at the moment. We are now surrounded by the ability to provide and/or read customer reviews instantly in social media, and the major retailers and service industries encourage consumer ratings now, too. If you can't find them there, check one of the many referral and review websites specifically designed for service reviews.

**Consumers Are Marketers**.   Beyond reviews and ratings, your company is no longer the sole determinant of the brand's perception or content. Who is? Consumers. They create massive content around brands today. Consumer relationships with brands dramatically shifted around 2008, when social media began dominating online interaction. The social media apparatus provided an opportunity to be on equal footing with brands, talking to them directly and using the facility of technology to share, comment, and like content. People now interact with brands in ways no one could have imagined when studying brand management in school just a short time ago. In those days, no one was welcome to use logos freely or produce anything for a brand that wasn't directly controlled by the corporate or advertising domain. Now it's the opposite. The brand belongs to the people. It's a brand free-for-all. With technology, consumers can take a screenshot, photograph, and disseminate content related to your brand whenever they like. And they do. Users now take time to submit photos classified with your hashtag on Instagram. There are no quality controls possible to monitor these personal photographs of brand interaction. Sometimes these interactions are not appropriate or even PG-rated. Welcome to a new age of democratic expression— one that includes the use/possible misuse of brand communication or branded experiences and products. A brand's Twitter tags can be applied to any thoughts, any political assertion, and any consumer satisfaction or complaint, and instead of litigating, a brand must now conduct itself as an interacter with its consumers.

A modern approach dictates that these interactions still qualify as part of a valid brand journey. Mechanisms such as a Facebook page put brands in direct dialogue with their customers and those customers' sharing of experiences, good and bad. It no longer matters what the official customer service hours are. A bank's Facebook page must be ready to deal with published content about its outrageous fees. A health food manufacturer might be called to task about its political contributions. An automotive manufacturer might be questioned about its factory standards. All of this happens in a very public domain with an audience of thousands who are sharing stories with clicks, in hyperspeed, 24/7, all around the world.

Even British Airways (BA) was taken to task with a paid social media promotion started by a customer's relative because of a lost bag.[1] After complaining on social media about the poor service, the consumer received a message that BA's social media monitoring is active only for certain hours and that a direct message should be sent to get a response at a later time. This spawned an interesting chain of events in response. Basically, the complainer paid to promote his tweet (like buying an ad buy) and targeted key BA markets. This generated a massive response of criticism for BA. What was a small problem that could have been easily addressed—a lost bag—became a huge social conversation of criticism fueled by a paid promotion to gain great reach in core targets. Now content by consumers is amplified like ads, by paying for coverage. It's not the first time people have paid to complain, but its easy now, its dynamic and powerful, and it reminds us of the use of our content in brand conversations and the expectations of consumers in service and on social media channels.

The fact is, everyone is more creative and expressive thanks to the Internet. Photography apps have turned everyone with a camera phone (i.e., everyone) into Andy Warhol or Ansel Adams. God help us! Clickable filters and photo editing tools democratize the ability to produce highly engaging images. Free (and robust!) blogging platforms give everyone the chance to be a published author and write about anything. Anyone can post editorial content and wax poetic about anything. Scores of blogs exist solely to offer reviews of products and services to specific subsets of customers: daddy blogs, crafter blogs, single mom blogs, parents of twins, gay auto enthusiasts, cosplay fans, furries, plushies, and many, many more. People start social media campaigns to save TV shows from cancellation. There are blogs dedicated specifically to a single TV program and recapping episodes of that show. There exist lively discussions among fans that can go on for pages and sometimes will include input from that show's writers and actors. People are creating and consuming content faster than ever before. This is a massive shift and cannot be avoided or stopped. Instead, evolve. Continue your shift from brand control to brand enablement. Build in the ability for greater participation through the creation of worlds and immersive experiences.

**Consumers Have Spidey Sense.** Now that you are connecting with the power of experience, let's understand why experience is so important. We must open our minds to one glaring, big, fat fact: In this information age, *there are no secrets*. This is truly an always-on world with anything you need at the click of a key, a mouse, or more likely, a tap and swipe across of a finger or two. Being hyperconnected brings an automatic by-product: increased transparency. Consumers feel, they sense, everything they need to know about a brand in approximately 4 seconds. Think about how this is true in your own life. Imagine you've traveled far, far away; you don't speak the language or know much about the culture. You walk into a mall and simply look around, determining which initial stores to visit. As soon as you step near the entrance of any store, you can very quickly determine whether that store is "right" for you or for your mom, whether it's upscale or downscale, whether they care about quality, whether they care about their customers, and so on. Consumers subconsciously arrive at these conclusions through the use of all of our senses, especially our sixth sense or, what we half jokingly call Spidey sense.

The reason customers want experiences rather than ads is rooted in basic human nature. We are all constantly writing, rewriting, editing, and conspiring about the story of ourselves. It's the one story. It's the one thing that you're tuned into all the time. You're never tuned out of your story, except for when you want to jump into a different story—like when you watch movies or read books or play video games. That is when people can escape from themselves and actively suspend reality. It is human nature to live from the concept of me, me, me—not just your customers, but all of us. Our minds are constantly assessing: "What's in it for me?" "How do I see myself in that car?" "How will someone else see me in that job?" If you could listen to the conversation that goes on in other people's heads, 90 percent of the conversations you'd hear would be about them, not about what's happening in the room, not about some higher-order thing. Everyone is involved in the journey of me.

Storytelling gurus know that the main ingredient in preparing great stories that connect with audiences is to make sure the audience finds themselves in the story. That makes it relatable. Whether your plot is overcoming a monster, a journey of survival, or love lost, it doesn't matter.  When people read a book, watch a movie, or hear a story, regardless of medium or format, it is imperative that they see themselves in the story. It doesn't matter if they see their aspirations or even see their flaws or their demons; they just need to see some aspect of themselves in the story. That is the power of story. You, as a business or brand, simply cannot make a more powerful connection than to literally become part of your customer's story. It's really that simple.

**Experience-Based Differentiation vs. Product Differentiation.** Clients generally come to us from one of two camps. Camp 1 recognizes and subscribes to the power of experience-based differentiation as a competitive advantage. Camp 2 arrives because of their concern regarding the ability to remain competitive and meet consumer expectations; they want to *find or leverage a product or service edge over competitors.* When working in camp 2, we seize the opportunity to delve into research that will help us best understand a particular consumer's expectations and behaviors. In this camp we also get to help consumers envision their shift into focusing on experiences. Sometimes we find consumer expectations actually exceed current possibilities. As an example, today customers of a retail chain would expect that if they purchased a product from an online store, they would certainly be able to drive to a physical store, walk inside, and return that product. This seems like a perfectly logical expectation for a customer to have. "Isn't this the same company I dealt with online?" they would ask themselves. The reality of operationalizing this simple customer expectation within that retail chain could be monumental. The retailer may need to connect things such as inventory systems together that were never designed for this. Who gets credit for the sale? The manager of the store or the woman responsible for the company website? How do you keep track of inventory across locations? A simple customer expectation could actually create havoc in their world. Some companies see these efforts to connect experiences as non–revenue generating and deprioritize them. Others see it as an expense that is a "necessary evil" in order to keep up with what other retail chains are doing and move forward with little urgency. The smart ones understand that creating great experiences can often offer you the competitive edge you are looking for.

Now jump back over to camp 1. These folks look for differentiated experiences that can be used to leapfrog the competition and lead the relevancy curve. A brand can lose its luster and need to be reinvigorated, which is more often than not something that's handled through advertising. But a business can also start becoming irrelevant when the product or the experience around the product or service becomes irrelevant. The example here is the Disney versus Hanna-Barbera story. One brand said it was in the business of *family entertainment*.[2] If this brand had just stuck with Mickey Mouse cartoons but never evolved into being the Disney of today, it could never have made that leap or that evolution. But when a similar brand defines itself as an *animation company*, then you can see the missed opportunities Hanna-Barbera had.[3] This context clearly displays an important distinction for how big brands are becoming irrelevant. Think about Blockbuster. There was one on every corner, while many mom-and-pop video rental places went out of business. In its heyday, they may have felt as though they took over the world. And now? If they would've just seen what else was changing, Netflix, Roku, or Hulu could've been their idea. All they had to do was ask customers about their worlds and pay attention. They didn't have to be geniuses; they just had to study consumers. This is why our focus on experiences, differentiated experiences, takes you into ethnography, social anthropology, product development, experience design, and innovation—it takes you into a world that gets deeply informed. People's behaviors and expectations change, and they change fast; look no further than technological innovation as the biggest catalyst to those changes. Pay attention to consumer tech evolution if you want to predict consumer behavior. If you're just in the business of making ads, you're more like Blockbuster, just trying to wrangle more people into that store on the corner. You lose the plot. You lose your place. You lose your relevance. You lose your business.

## Ladbrokes: *Creating a new world Storyscape from an old world of betting*
CASE STUDY

**The Old World of Betting**. Ladbrokes is one of the oldest betting companies in Britain. Not only does it possess a pastoral, equine history, it's a company that's helped popularize betting in England. Since 1886 they've been number one. Imagine a ubiquity that at times had more retail spaces than the country's largest grocery chain; that's around 3,000 high street stores. Betting was a foot traffic culture—bets were placed in person at stores or racetracks for more than 100 years. Ladbrokes' marketing was all about offers in odds. But advertising "5 to 1" or "7 to 5" was a message only savvy bettors and mathematicians understood. For everybody else, it was like a foreign language. And "everybody else" was a large market share that the entire category was vying to attract. Soon enough the offers became about freebies. "Sign up and get 10 free bets." These offers relied heavily on television. TV ads about free bets and odds air on British television about as often as that insurance gecko airs in America. That's a lot of TV spots about betting. That's a lot of TV spots pushing price-based differentiation and the inevitable road to commoditization. Everything ran on this course until about 2009, when digital opportunities changed the game for them forever.

**No One Likes to Lose Top Spot**. Ladbrokes had lost its coveted number one ranking to its competitor. It was losing its typical customers to old age and not attracting new consumers, the ones who do virtually everything online or on their mobile devices, rarely in person. The brand continued to appeal to financial rewards. It would attract a customer seeking free bets and then lose that customer to the next company offering free bets.

It just amounted to the consumer chasing the free bets offer; there was no real emotional connection between the Ladbrokes brand and its consumer. This reinforces the challenge of price- or value-based differentiation. We had to find a better way.

**Finding a New Way to Connect with Consumers.** We analyzed the Ladbrokes business strategy, which at the time hadn't included a meaningful digital perspective. We conducted research on betting behavior and the emotion of betting. Why do people bet? They bet to feel smarter, to enjoy intellectual reward. They also bet as part of a social mechanism, with friends or office pools. But one great thing we uncovered in our examination was that no single company was really exploiting the key emotional component of why people bet; it's exciting! No betting brand was telling the story of excitement. We convinced Ladbrokes that excitement was the key and no one else was doing it. We had found a powerful territory for emotional story differentiation. We also established how we had to deliver that excitement and what we needed to create more exciting experiences. We began by building the massive, intelligent technology platform so trading could occur in real-time—exciting! We then created a mobile offering that enabled betting in real-time anywhere—exciting! We essentially used technology to create real time products and services with advanced betting intelligence for smarter dynamic betting—exciting! We then delivered communication that built the story of excitement. Here is a story and Experience Space that could change the game for consumers. As an example, the Ladbrokes bettor could wager on more than 700 possibilities in every single football match, not just the fulltime or halftime scores—exciting!

**A Story System Built on Excitement.** Rather than trying to plaster the Ladbrokes story everywhere with the excited character from the television ad, we used the Organizing Idea of "Game On" to guide how we designed the Story System. By having communications and experience design teams together, we gave the messaging more dimension. For example, every time the bettor hit the Bet button, it would flash "Game On" to reinforce the excitement and the brand story. But that's just the surface of it all. We're not just talking excitement; we're offering excitement. We're letting the bettor participate in the narrative so that it doesn't even matter who wins; it becomes about the bettor being able to participate in this unprecedented way. Bettors can continue participating from wherever they are sitting. Ladbrokes has redefined its betting category as "live odds" betting. Ladbrokes' customers now bet on a robust online platform updated in real time with intelligence on every possible betting outcome. Consumers receive Ladbrokes alerts on odds that change in real time based on what's happening in the game that moment. And they can act on it via a mobile phone. The "betting store," so to speak, is now in the pocket. As an example of the power in the Storyscape, in a game of soccer/football, if a player's just taken off or just got on the pitch or if someone missed a goal or shot a goal right before the commercial break, the Ladbrokes TV spot will air an offer specifically reflecting true-to-life game events—yes, in real time. That's a dynamic story and experience that is connected, because at the same time, someone at the game can be alerted, enabling that person to bet live. Or as another example, say legend Wayne Rooney takes the pitch a few moments before an ad break; the Ladbrokes spot will pull a live odd for Wayne Rooney to score for, say, 100 pounds and promote it. It all adds a new dimension of excitement to the soccer/football experience and mostly to what it means to participate. The communication and the betting live anywhere; the bettor is immersed within the story regardless of whether there to see the game in person, watching on TV, or hanging out at the family picnic just reading the odds.

Creating the world of immersive experience for Ladbrokes was achieved through real connected thinking. We had a strategist examine the category for insight. We used psychologists to define and understand how consumers want to participate with the brand, not as "users" the way many digital shops like to consider their target audience, but as people. Our media research group studied *all* marketing channels, not just TV. Our technology experts developed systems to deliver new connected experiences—apps, platforms, interfaces, and much more—to strengthen the product with the backbone of the world. We used writers and art directors to tell the stories in resonant and accessible and oh so exciting ways.

**A Changed Business.** We started out with trying to make an old brand relevant again, and the result was that we totally changed the Experience Space. With account sign-ups increasing 65 percent, sports betting turnover in digital up 34.5 percent, and live, in-play betting up 34.2 percent, we certainly shifted the needle, returning Ladbrokes to their number one spot.

And the story is resonating on an emotional level, too. Ad tracking "reflects the excitement of betting" increased to 54 percent, versus 37 percent, for the average competitor, while brand preference has increased 33 percent to reclaim the leadership spot. And the conversation continues, with social media monitoring showing Ladbrokes is three times more talked about than its closest rival.

All up, Storyscape for Ladbrokes has truly created a new world, a world of experience, a world of participation, a world where the brand is part of the consumer's story. Game On. Results like these prove that when we as business leaders stay focused on the immersive experience and relevant stories by truly understanding the consumer, we renew our membership as master of ceremonies and we appreciate the financial benefits that follow.

**Technology Is an Enabling Tool.** Technology affords us lots of supercool things in this life. When you boil it all down, many of these supercool things would probably be found under the heading of "wants" versus "needs." However, rampant expectations means that the needs list drafted a major player with its addition of mobile banking. We now have the ability to take a photo of legal tender, a check, and send that photo up into space. It then comes back down, lands on a computer monitor, and that's good enough for the bank to say, in an authentic drive-through teller voice, "Okay, we'll add this amount to your account and update your balance accordingly." Sheer brilliance based on practicality. This technology certainly provides a convenience value and the comfort factor of no longer having to interact with the process-oriented, transaction-based bank teller. Who would have ever imagined the almighty dollar being used in such a way? And now that we can deposit a check by taking a photo of it, our world crumbles that moment when the mobile banking software hiccups and will not take our deposit. *What do you mean the photo doesn't work today? Are you serious? I have to get in the car and drive to a branch. They are sooooo going to hear about this when I get there!* Power to the people. Of course, it is not technology alone that allows this virtual transaction. Behind the curtain, there exists another form of creativity, one that requires "systems thinking," a keen understanding of the human experience and the imagination to reinvent or reimagine how the world could or should work. That said, these ideas have little value unless you can make them real, which requires some tools. Technology is the new paper and pencil that drives this.

Clearly, the platforms of delivery have gotten a whole lot more interesting, vast, fast, kinetic, and kinesthetic with the recent advancements in technology. Technology enables connection of individuals on a mass scale, so affinity and community can be established more easily and faster than ever before. As a result, the speed of adoption and innovation can be faster and niche groups can be large scale. We have been preaching about the powerful emotional connections that can be made between brands and their customers though experience, but you may ask, "What's so emotional? What's so personal about technology? Zeros and ones are not exactly warm and fuzzy, right?" Well that's exactly the point of this book. In the conventional world the storytellers are entrusted with crafting communications, and the product or operations folks are charged with developing the products and systems. We believe those barriers need to be demolished. Any good chief marketing officer (CMO) wants some influence on the product experience. You can't run BMW and be out there telling the world, "This is the Ultimate Driving Machine"[4] but then make a crappy car. That's not going to work for long. In his book *Designing Business,* Clement Mok wrote about how the experience is the brand. We wholeheartedly believe that as well.

We all need to recognize that in this digital storytelling era—a brand now has the power to create an experience with its customer, who then wants to be part of the story, as opposed to just being told your brand story. This is an important distinction, and whenever any of us recognizes this opportunity, we should opt for creating immersive and memorable experiences more often. Having an experience with your brand is the connection that consumers desire and expect. And remember, actions speak louder than words; experiences are more powerful, and there's no substitute for the real thing. Make your experiences authentic.

After reviewing marketplace and expectation changes, it's easy to agree that consumers seek interaction, engagement, and participation with brands. And although experiences are the opportunity, they cannot exist in isolation. To create brand value and meaningful relationships, experiences cannot afford to be isolated; they need to be part of the brand story line, but more than that, they need to be part of a Story System. Therefore, our focus should be on more than just the power of story, and more than the power of experience: You need to begin *creating worlds*.

# BRAVE NEW WORLDS

*Moving from Storytelling to Storyscaping*

# BRAVE NEW WORLDS

*Moving from Storytelling to Storyscaping*

If you read the Introduction, you'll remember how we shared our belief that story*telling* (creating ads) is only about one-third of the recipe today. It's in the other two-thirds (creating worlds) where the real customer connection happens through shared experiences. In other words, to increase results, we must focus on creating a *world* where immersive experiences connect people with brands. As part of creating the right *world,* the old way of marketing (creating ads) becomes just part of the system for sustainability, brand loyalty, and possibly even survival. We cannot have one without the other, so it is far less effective with only one-third and not the other two thirds.

**Your College Years Were Not a Total Waste.** In other current marketing books and blogs, you may be getting the message that it's a new world, that the past doesn't matter, that you should leave behind everything you used to do. During agency pitches, you may be getting the message that digital is here, social media is the way and everything else is dead. On news channel interviews, you may be witnessing some bickering between the new school calling the old school a dinosaur who has fallen and the old school retorting about longevity and wisdom while they shrug off their opponent as a passing fad. Well, we do not subscribe to the belief that it's an either/or scenario. We feel it would be unwise to forget everything you once knew. What you understand from your past ways of creating, planning, and placing your brands, your products and your services is still very valid. If and when you use the old ways, they come into play after you've created your *world,* and you are ready to tell people how to find your connection points into that world. We encourage you to realize that the battle of new media versus old media does not really matter; winning or losing that battle of definition will not effect real change or bring results. What matters is your willingness and ability to broaden your mind and evolve. Most people who pick up this book will already be sitting on one or the other side of the old media/new media wall; it seems few people are in the middle. We think that is a real problem. Instead of trying to define which school of thought you subscribe to, shift into the act of creating a world and just watch; you may be amazed to find that battle dissolving before your eyes because it will become very apparent that there is room for both new and old media, new and old ways. As we said before, it's an evolution more than a revolution. The hard part is figuring out which old tools to keep, which to discard, and which new ones to add to your trusty tool belt. We can't give you a specific answer on that because it's different for everyone. What we will do is show you a foolproof way to arrive at an answer for yourself.

We have all worked the old way of telling a story with just the written word and know there is a definite craft to that. We've also worked the angle of adding moving pictures to take story to an even more interesting place, and there is a craft to that as well. Now, with fast advances and vast benefits in digital technology and media fragmentation, many companies are having trouble bridging the gap between old and new. Our belief is that shifts in consumer behavior and expectations pose the single biggest threat and in doing so also provide the biggest opportunity for business today. The world is changing fast; take advantage of it. Imagine owning a travel agency, record store, bookstore, video rental, independent insurance agency, car dealership, even restaurant; how has your business changed over the past five years? Many have failed while some have flourished. Ask yourself something about the winners and survivors. Did changing their positioning (story) alone help, or did they win by changing their business, or both? This is where business is truly suffering and names we didn't expect to fall have crumbled.

To significantly reduce this challenge, we at SapientNitro have learned that it's a matter of shifting focus away from your competition and focusing deep on what your customers' future expectations and behaviors may look like. A big communication idea alone can treat the symptoms of irrelevancy in the short term, but unless you at least meet consumer expectations for experience, you will eventually lose out to someone who does. Advertising is important, yes, but today you must move beyond sole reliance on its ability to drive your business. Spend your time crafting a brand world that includes communications and beyond, where all facets of the business are connected and working in tandem. We say, "Create the right world, and success will follow." When your world is well defined, cooperatively created, and connected systematically, then the results are impressive!

At the highest level, we have touched on the role story plays in helping us make sense of the world. We have highlighted the power of experience as a way to create personal stories for people. Now we are going to explore the concept of Experience Space (world) versus media plan as our canvas in an effort to show you can start to see how we will build connections. We believe we need to start by poking a ton of holes in the advertising industry's media centric view of the world. We believe this myopia is what gets in the way of agencies and advertisers creating worlds. Even the premise of *bought*, *owned*, and *earned* media—although smarter and more inclusive—is still somewhat broken because it falls short of reality. See, the last time we checked, we found that a consumer's world consists of more than media alone, and you sure as hell can't expect to go into a media planning database, punch in a few data points, and have it spit out a map of the world around that consumer, including influences, behaviors, and preferences—it is still all focused on media consumption and reach, two important data points if you want to push a message one way, but hardly what you fully need to create a connected experience. Having an experience with your brand is the connection that consumers desire and expect. So, we have to reinvent connections planning to give it to them.

**Worlds by Design.** We've been showing you how stories are the threads people use to make sense of the world we live in. Naturally, a story that glides across physical and virtual space and is connected through emotional space is sure to make even greater sense of (and connection to) *everything*. This is what we call the Experience Space, and it effectively defines a world. To fully describe a world is much more thought provoking: Worlds are more powerful than words. Worlds contain stories **th**at people want to be part of. Worlds are created through a Story System; they ca**nn**ot be developed through a mere story line or media plan. Worlds are composed **of** multiple interesting spaces where people enjoy interacting with brands. Worlds provide opportunities for people to connect with brands in immersive and cooperative ways. Worlds have intraconnectivity and regenerating energy and live for action. Worlds are guided, and worlds are free flowing. Worlds are where we draw a real connection between communications and commerce. Worlds are, well, worlds are where brands and consumers coexist.

To better understand this *world* we speak of, consider it the Experience Space, the canvas upon which brands and people get to connect, engage, and play. You design this Experience Space to intentionally cut across physical space and virtual space, and you connect it through emotional space. Let's explore this. Say you're sitting in a chair in your office, with a desk, a computer, and all the typical office stuff. You're holding onto and reading this book. That describes one dimension—the physical space. Simultaneously, there's a monologue going on in your head, "I gotta make sure I send that proposal off to Janet so she can review it and get it over to Quentin; we really need to close that deal. . . . Andre's birthday is tomorrow. . . . I hope the weather holds out for our road trip this weekend . . ." All this while you're online checking the status of your home owner's insurance policy, reading an e-mail from your boss, and scanning closing prices on the Dow. This is the dimension known as the virtual space. We concurrently live in physical space and in our own minds. Our ability to bounce in and out of these different dimensions defines the always-on environment we all live and work in today. This is why you can no longer get away from having both a great product and a great story and why you need to create shared stories through the power of immersive experiences within your brand world. Utilize both the power of story and the necessity of experience to differentiate your brand. Remember everything we do must account for the overlap of the physical, virtual, and always-present emotional space—be it online, offline, or in work mode. Those are ideas of the past.

**Widen Your Experience Space.** One of the things we discovered here is a capability we had never been exposed to in the traditional agency space. We never even knew this existed. The hidden treasures we discovered evolved from some investments Sapient's founders had made back in our tech consulting days. Jerry and Stuart believed that clients would spend tons of effort building systems that people would never adopt or would simply not get the most value from. These guys believed strongly that great design was a huge business advantage, with creative directors constantly evaluating advertising, as if it's the air we breathe. Often we observe work that is rather entertaining, clever, and funny or that really draws on the emotional space. But rarely do those works explain the role of the brand or the role of the product effectively. We see work that is pretty interesting or compelling, but it's simply conveying a linear narrative. Even those ads that we love for their entertaining and memorable aspects, we don't often recall the associated brand so, in the end, how do those entertaining ads connect to everything else that company does? What is the point if we can't deliver that experience at the store? Zoom out your experience lens. Search for new possibilities to connect with more than one dimension. The former process of finding the highest reach and frequency and placing a linear ad buy no longer cuts it. Connection points exist in many, many more areas than just through your media; they are everywhere! Remember, this relates all communication and what you communicate through your actions, which determines people's perception of you. Each one of your communications can be considered a connection point! Do you think the employees of your company have (and share) a perception of your brand? Of course they do! And since they have the most personal and most frequent engagement with it, why not start internally? How do your employees view you? How in line are your human resources policies? How is the turnover rate? Do employees believe in and act from your company Purpose, or are they out blowing the whistle on your weak points? Start tying your internal actions to the external image you wish to portray!

**Easier Entry to Market.** Fact: Technology has dissolved many former barriers around launching a brand. Over the past decade, the real estate and physical assets a business needed to acquire to get its brand to market ranged from between considerable and huge, and now it has worked its way down to home based. Before the new millennium, who discussed start-up businesses? Historically, big companies launched new brands, and even with those powerful driving engines, few survived. Small businesses could make a go if they capped themselves by geography. Their costs to produce, warehouse, advertise, and ship to perspective customers beyond that local range was simply too prohibitive. The barrier known as economies of scale, whereby a smaller business strapped for the ability to produce large enough quantities to compete with the big guys, is less of a threat these days because they have more outlets for funding and more partners who help bear the load. Technology has shrunk overhead by millions of dollars and offered considerable savings appreciated by all business sizes. Freed-up resources and increased speed to market helped us all.

The road of an entrepreneur was once a lonely one—but no more. Entrepreneurs are more connected than ever, sharing deep-dive plans and experiences of success and failure. Start-up networking events have become worth their weight in gold, gaining direct conversation and answers at the conception stage of the new business life yet to be developed. There are even networking groups who focus on learning from the mistakes of others or who rehash and resuscitate solid start-up ideas that originally failed. Plentiful are the categories of networking groups meeting in local homes or across the globe, all steeped in a very important and new overall theme: transparency. Transparency is becoming a consistent and comfortable theme. There seems to be a new focus on helping your brothers and sisters, and in doing so, the realization that everybody wins. Examine the word *community*— *comm* (common and/or communication) + *unity*. No coincidence here. Networking is uniting entrepreneurs in their common goals and communication around those goals. It is easy to do this now with the choices in contact platforms bringing human connection face to face with built-in video cameras, offered in many cases at no cost. Perhaps we recognize this in the technology industry because so many of these entrepreneurs are accustomed to building on other people's ideas. Maybe unifying energy is subtly rippling out from the teams in India, the country that brought Yoga (which means union) to the rest of the world. These ripples may be worth paying attention to as we continue to restructure the way we approach marketing and even run our businesses. Maybe after tucking our daily *Wall Street Journal* safely into the recycle bin, we should visit our local New Age bookstore, where we can gain a brief, meaningful lesson on the underlying energy of oneness, cooperation, and community. Peruse the pages of *A New Earth*, by German author Eckhart Tolle.[1] After all, there must be some credence to his message if Oprah invested not just by inviting him as a show guest but by producing a full-on webinar series[2] where readers could be assisted with absorbing his message of cooperation and oneness through supplemental workbooks, additional exercises, resources, and tips for spiritual awakening. This webcast called, "Oprah and Eckhart's A New Earth" began as part of her bookclub, where they offered one class per chapter. The series is still available at: http://www.oprah.com/oprahsbookclub/A-New-Earth-Are-You-Ready-to-be-Awakened. Greater transparency and authentic cooperation both lend a hand to easier entry to market.

On the other side of this coin, the challenge is that low barriers of entry also create breeding grounds for increased competition. This is not good or bad; it just changes how you look at (manage) it. Increased competition requires us to tone up our story—continually tailoring messaging to be clear-cut and sharply effective in order to cut through the masses and part the waters.

Experience standards have also risen, and consumers want to feel as if they are in your story. They need to experience brands and even the businesses behind those brands more kinesthetically. Brand engrossment is the goal, and the old ways of full-court press and big pushes just don't work to engross. These customers who are attracted during a big push are less likely to still be using that product in the years to come. Instead, become the wise, fine-tuned athlete who trains with strategy, focus, and dedication, confidently knowing that the slower burn leads to best overall results. The donor-fund projects that focus on a short-term, fast sale target actually lead attention away from the slower burn of satisfying customers—where they could be enjoying ongoing engagement, usage, and the incredible engine of positive word of mouth. May we recommend and insert a story to help? Reread the story of the tortoise and the hare, remembering "slow and steady wins the race."

**That's Some Kind of Fragment You Got There.** Everyone's been talking about how media fragmentation is what is creating challenges in the communication space, but they're all wrong. Our argument is that it's actually experience fragmentation. It's the fact that marketing is no longer linear, and it's certainly not predictable. Go back to the early 1980s, when there was a script and it evolved, but only slightly. Take prime-time TV, for instance. We could rely on audiences being creatures of habit. We could predict, with Nielsen's help, that most nights, most members of the family would be sitting on the couch in front of the TV eating dinner and watching their collective favorite network series. Similarly, in the world of radio, we relied on broadcasting our ads during commute times to and from work. There was a linear experience of reaching a specific audience on certain days at certain times. This is how most communications strategy and media buys were designed. You could actually choose one medium that made the most sense for that audience or product and place it at a specific period of time, and everything could be created with a beginning, middle, and end and actually end with a full stop.

There are a finite number of eyeballs and hours. People have only so much leisure time, and the concern has been focused on how the more time they spend on the Internet, the increasingly less time they'll watch TV, the increasingly less time they'll read the paper, and the increasingly less time they'll listen to the radio. What has actually happened is the amount of TV time that people are spending hasn't really changed. But there's been a dramatic change in time that people spend on the Internet or mobile devices. Newspapers—screwed, but not solely because of readership declines, but because of revenue streams—have evaporated virtually overnight. Why? Because the thing that made the most money for a newspaper was the classifieds, and eBay, Craigslist, and the fact that you can get everything online has made the classified section irrelevant. It had less to do with consumption; the readership issue was an older problem. What has really gotten hammered are publications that are broad and not highly curated, because now we do our own curating. Consumers jump around and get whatever we want. Therefore, you can't have linear stories; you need nonlinear Story Systems.

**People Are Walking, Breathing Filters.** What's interesting when you start to look at that whole world is that we are simply consuming more stuff. No media is really stealing share away from another media, with the exception of print. We've somehow found more time, which is bizarre, but it's true and it's because of our evolved multitasking. Everyone is working while eating breakfast, lunch, and dinner. People are watching TV while surfing, shopping, or status-izing on their notebook, tablet, or smartphone. What happens now is we are having all these connected experiences and we're moving in and out of each of them all of the time. Can someone figure out how to make sense of or connect them? There's much more to learn about this whole other world around what they call transmedia storytelling or non linear narratives, where each bit of interaction plays a role in the overall story. Call it what you want; for us it's a Story System.

One of the more common questions we hear is, "How do you break through the clutter?" In most cases, the common answer offers something about needing a better story and needing to be more strategic with media choices and of course that you need to zig when everyone else zags. But, not everyone agrees with these popular concepts. A handful of big-time successful global companies talk about it differently. They believe there is no clutter and that we as consumers are not overwhelmed. They believe we are actually in control of what we do and do not pay attention to. That connects back to our "Spidey sense." We are now very sophisticated machines that filter stuff out. We only home in on the information we care about. Instead of it being about getting your message seen through the clutter, this philosophy states the importance of getting consumers to let you in and getting them to care. This goes back to the idea of being Purpose driven, rather than just "producing and selling another blue teddy bear," as Dame Vivienne Westwood puts it. Consumers filter you by asking themselves in a nanosecond, "Why should I let you be part of my world?" That's the question that consumers are asking. And the louder (story-yelling) you try to break through the clutter, the more likely it is they will ignore you, because you're just another "nox" in a sea of obnoxious. It's paradoxical. No one actually wants to see ads, yet there are ads that we actually seek out and pass to other people asking, "Did you see this?"

**The Brand as Content Creator.** Today's consumer is not only a purveyor of voluminous content but also capable of absorbing and, indeed, desirous of more, fresh content all the time. This puts the brand in the unique position of being a constant supplier of editorial content. Owing to the now necessary Twitter accounts, Pinterest boards, Facebook pages, and Instagram feeds, brands have a new responsibility of creating editorial content to keep their followers engaged. The essence of the brand used to be defined through design and product offering and now has expanded to include the brand's ability to curate and create content—and deliver it almost daily.

**Blending the Power of Two.** In the previous chapter, we highlighted the power of experience by reliving your first kiss. We also introduced the importance of experience-based differentiators to help lift your brand. Both are great tools; both have a shelf life. The aha! of Storyscaping is that it takes these two tools and combines their power. A differentiated product or offering or service is typically easy to copy. Your department store offers valet parking, and in two weeks, every other department store can have valet parking. The fact that you did it first, and that differentiated your experience, will give you some advantage, but that advantage is fleeting. Instead, create opportunities to say something about your brand. That's more sustainable because you can reinforce it with other behaviors that support your ethos and Purpose. If you're doing something just because everyone else is, that's where it will fall short.

More brands exist now than ever. The superhighway lanes that lead consumers to these brands continue to sophisticate, articulate, and re-create access galore. There is a sea of options for search engines—one brand so powerful and popular it became *the* category verb, now living as a listing in the dictionary, and it continues to direct the world's population toward their desired answers and to all other brands: the power of Google-generated search, an entirely transformational category of marketing. The Internet, with its spawned digital ancillaries, is the world's largest art gallery. This gallery is filled to the brim—no centimeter unhung—with constantly changing canvases for storytelling. Reviewed more often than The Rolling Stones and as cluttered as Times Square, the challenge continues to be the ability of uncovering engaging content.

The solution here is a more strategic application of stories as a means to make sense of the complexity. Remember the idea that stories help us make sense of the world around us. In a world that continues to grow more complex, we could use a better story. The days of disruption as a tactic are in the dust. Not every channel can deliver the levels of engagement we desire. Try to drop the concept of "two clicks and they're out" and open up, being okay with the concept that it makes good sense to designate some channels as signposts or roundabouts that effectively transfer the consumer to the most engaging content and the transactional engine. Face it, this is no longer a linear process; we don't know what time they will arrive at the art gallery or which canvas will capture their engagement. Therefore, it is imperative that all your touch points serve a purpose in the Story System.

### Does Technology Inspire the Story, or Does the Story Inspire Technology?

Sometimes it feels as if new technologies are the driving force in the director's chair for most every transformational scene in our business history. What do you come up with when you ask yourself the pivotal question, "Does the story drive technology, or does technology drive the story?" Although easier to prove than the age-old question "Which came first, the chicken or the egg," this seemingly simple question is an important one to ponder when you're developing your business strategy. Take James Cameron, for example, he had written *Avatar* more than 15 years before he made the movie.[3] The script remained in a drawer for that long simply because he knew technology did not exist yet to deliver the story through film in a credible and compelling way. In that case, he waited until it did, whereas in other cases, he had ponied up and invented new technologies and techniques to get the right effect.[4] In those cases his vision for the story inspired the tech. The swing camera was one such technology. The head rig he used to record facial expressions was also one of his solutions. Conversely, there are a number of examples in which a new technology he was made aware of inspired a new vision for a story, picture the liquid monster in *Abyss*.

To drive this point home let's delve deeper into Cameron's work; let's talk movies! Remember how, in their day, the following movies were considered the absolute in cutting edge: *Terminator* (I and II), *Aliens*, *Titanic*, and of course, who could forget *Avatar*? James Cameron is the filmmaker who championed these blockbusters and who some might say stands in a league of his own (a league he created from his sci-fi technology generators). Cameron is a storyteller first, but he's also a systems thinker, a creative technologist, and inventor to boot. These connected capabilities have propelled his reputation for stunning visual effects, created through technology so advanced that it was not previously conceptualized, let alone constructed.

To re-create and tell his version of the 1912 sinking of the *Titanic* story in a way where audiences felt a part of it—using realistic visual effects—it took imagination and effort of titanic proportions. Cameron had a special studio built in Mexico that featured a 17-million-gallon water tank and 775-foot replica of the *Titanic*.[5] Authenticity in this story called for Cameron himself to deep-sea dive 2.5 miles below the surface of the North Atlantic waters, where he could see the actual remains of Titanic, not just to get a little peek to pique his inspiration. No. The 1997 *Titanic* filming required him to make 12 submersible dives to the wreck itself, two and a half miles down in the North Atlantic. Years later, Cameron went back for more. In all, he made 33 dives to *Titanic*, logging more hours on that ship than Captain Smith himself.[6] In preparation for his 2001 expedition to the *Titanic* wreck, Cameron developed revolutionary fiber-spooling mini Remotely Operated Vehicles (ROVs)—tethered underwater robots that allow the vehicle's operator to remain in a safe environment while the ROV captured findings in the fragile environment. His team's historic exploration of *Titanic's* interior was the subject of his 3-D IMAX film, *Ghosts of the Abyss*. This is an example of how this story drove this technology. These robots that captured the authentic footage to bring *Titanic* to life are *story driven*. Fast-forward to 2009, the release of *Avatar* introduced audiences to more unprecedented technology, known as performance capture.[7] Cameron works from the understanding that even science fiction—although based on fantasy—has to be built on a foundation of reality. This premise was carried throughout the filmmaking process—into the assisting minds and hands that created *Avatar*. The creature design team scoured books of animal biology, animal anatomy, and even texture books offering the aesthetic feel of everything from the back of a tortoise to the area on a Horn Bill that lies between its beak and its bill to the feel of a poison dart frog.[8] This team used nature's resourcefulness and imagination to fuel their creations, which is why the creatures in the film feel real. Cameron understands that audiences don't have to believe that it's 100 percent photo real or that these creatures actually exist. What he has to prove is that they are *emotional* creatures. Emotion—the element in stories that makes an audience connect—still applies and must appear through any given technology employed.[9] These imagined, yet realistic and emotional creatures, brought to life through performance capture are story driven. Two huge films, two different stories, two unique approaches, each with their own unique special effects, all where technology was secondary to the story and heart of the movie. After all was said and done with all of his industry-transforming films—the newest in computer-generated software manufactured marvels of visual wonders, the Academy donned their awards, and the Globes were gripped and redisplayed— Cameron stood by the story under it all.

Storyscaping is more than a philosophy; it is a methodology and approach that you can apply to your business today. We further define *Storyscaping* as a landscape of emotional and transactional experiences, where each connection inspires engagement with another, so the brand becomes part of the consumer's story. When you use the Storyscaping model, it will enable you to evolve your craft in a way that makes it easier to connect to the physical, virtual, and emotional Experience Space that surrounds the customer. We will help you move beyond making ads and into creating worlds where your story can become their story through shared experiences.

## Vail Resorts: *EpicMix Photo*
CASE STUDY

**Every Mountain Has a Story.** Since the 1960s, vacationers have skied at the iconic mountains that are part of the Vail Resorts collection. The desire to explore and share experiences is never ending on these majestic slopes. Traditionally, their personal journeys of triumph over nature were just that, personal and usually either just a memory or one backlit snapshot.

Understanding that technology was fast becoming a part of everybody's everyday journey, Vail Resorts released an interactive experience in 2010 called EpicMix.[10] If you were a guest at one of their then five different mountains, your lift pass came embedded with a RFID chip that automatically captures the guests on mountain experiences, allowing them to track vertical feet, earn pins, view trail maps, and access snow reports. It also provided the ability to share their stories socially on Facebook and Twitter both online and on the free Android and iPhone applications.

**Nature and Technology Join Forces.** Vail Resorts guests were now mobile and socially connected. They were socially connected, shooting, checking in, and sharing their comments right from the snow. So we helped Vail Resorts leverage a ripe opportunity for creating a world that started on the slopes, was disseminated by smartphones, and kept alive long after the vacation was over.

We knew that EpicMix could evolve with even greater appeal to its most valuable customers. We understood that the opportunity existed to transform what was traditionally an experience of random pieces on social channels into a world of engagement. To build this world, we helped Vail

Resorts organize itself around an Organizing Idea—Unleash the Mountain— and build a system for the guests' vacation story and their interaction with mountain adventures.

**Unleash the Mountain**. The immersive world of EpicMix Photo offers many connection points and ways to engage with the guest. If for every mountain there's a story, then for every story there are many, many images. Pro photographers are strategically stationed all over the resorts to capture everything from family portraits to deep powder and big air. Those images are automatically uploaded to guest accounts via the embedded chip in their lift passes. Guests can share these high-quality images for free, and doing so has been wildly popular. They can also order high-resolution prints as an added option. EpicMix digital pins encourage exploration of the mountain with people sharing that exploration online. The Collage feature is like an extreme scrapbook. Skiers and riders can share their entire experience with achievement pins and personal stats. Skiers can calculate total vertical feet skied on the trip and tally their best day from the data automatically tracked for them in their account. There is now a racing component (EpicMix Racing) that allows guests to race against friends, family, and even Lindsey Vonn, Four Time Overall World Cup Champion and Olympic Gold Medalist.[11] Guests can view their race times, earn medals, share their accomplishments, and get racing tips to up their game from the legend herself. It all plays out on a dynamic, Mondrian-style grid that encourages skiers and riders to stay in their mountain worlds long after they've left the mountain. And it stays there forever. A family can preserve a lifetime of ski vacation memories for generations.

**A Mountain of Experiences**. All of this was wrapped up in a beautiful design, a tightly integrated mobile-Web-social system, and a new user interface that even worked with gloves on! Most hospitality and entertainment businesses would be grateful for an e-mail address from a parting guest. Vail Resorts can proudly boast over 500,000 members of a community created from Storyscaping. This sort of engagement far supersedes expectations of traditional vacation brands. Perhaps the most staggering number, though, is the 180 million social post impressions generated by the Story System that is EpicMix.

*"Thank you Miss EpicMix Photographer. You are awesome. You have no idea how your expertise affected our family. Today was a dream three years and eight months in the making. You took the Christmas card photo today. THANK YOU!"*

—Vail EpicMix Guest

*". . . EpicMix is expanding into photography in a big way, and it's a significant step not just for the company, but for skiers' and snowboarders' experiences with their sport. . .Photo is the big change, and here, Vail is out front of Disney and almost every other vacation destination that does pro photography."*

—Wired Magazine

In your own life, you've witnessed and experienced and can now fully realize the universal power of digital technology. Just add some of the power of tech to leverage and deepen the immersive experiences people can have with your brand. Get them involved in your story, and at the same time, they will be creating their own story *and sharing it.* Open up now, and set your sights on creating a brand *world.* Visualize this world as the Experience Space where you connect with the right people, for the right reason, in the right way, and in the right time. Within your world, imagine connection points where people can have an immersive experience with your brand. Imagine these connection points are strategically designed in a way that enables people to create their own stories as they jump into your world and become part of your brand.

In summary, a brand must have a story that matters. By "matters," we mean a story that is founded on a real Purpose and values that are shared with consumers. To have a story that matters, a brand must not only speak authentically, but *be* and behave authentically. And to become part of their customer's worlds and personal stories, a brand needs to create memorable experiences for them that are effective across all shared interactions. To accomplish this, you must delve deep into your customer's world, uncover ways to become part of it, avoid the distraction of competitors, and learn to tell your story through experience, not just words and pictures. That's it. And you're wondering, how ever can we do this? Storyscaping is the secret, and the next section of this book is dedicated to showing you how.

# PART TWO

*Storyscaping Immersive Experiences for Powerful Brand and Consumer Connections*

# THE STORYSCAPING MODEL

*Deciphering the Code to Creating Worlds*

# THE STORYSCAPING MODEL

*Deciphering the Code to Creating Worlds*

Roll up your sleeves; we're about to examine the lay of the Storyscaping land. In Part Two, we will introduce and illustrate the structures, logic, terms, elements, pillars, and thinking that amalgamate an effective Storyscape. We will start with the model that illustrates how we codified the Storyscaping approach. This sets the frame for the following chapters, each of which covers in detail a section of the model. Ideally, you will walk away with a great understanding of how to begin thinking of your brand differently, marketing your business more effectively, and you'll gain actionable ideas you can walk away with and immediately begin to implement for overall greater business success. These principles are applicable to the 10-person start-up or the 10,000-person multinational business. They apply to new brands and old.

**Foundation for Real Success.** Success starts with setting goals. Otherwise, how do you determine your level of success? Storyscaping is based on the principle that we are trying to effectively connect organizations (brands) with people (consumers). This is achieved across the Experience Space through the creation of shared values and shared experiences by making shared stories that build participation. Therefore, defining and understanding the lay of the land where you are preparing to work is fundamental. This foundation has two parts. First, we pinpoint your desired consumers. Who are you trying to make connections with? Who are you trying to attract? Storyscaping is about making connections with both existing and new consumers with equal importance. Second, we seek and define the "consumer to brand" business/marketing challenge. This sets up what your goals need to be, what you want to achieve, and what success looks like. It should be both inspiring and meaningful for the business.

Whether you call them *consumers, guests, clients,* or *customers* does not matter; what matters is that you very clearly define who they are. And, at all costs, please avoid referring to or thinking of these people as an *audience* or *user*. Doing so implies that they are passive watchers of your story or users of utility, instead of being engaged and participatory. We are looking to create experiences beyond the story, immersive experiences that change behavior; therefore, "targeting an audience" sets up the wrong premise from the start. The fact that these people create so much of your content, have such powerful influence, and actually control their interaction within your Experience Space makes calling them an *audience* or *user* just plain wrong. No matter what label you reference (*consumers, guests,* etc.), please always keep in mind that these are people—human beings. These are the very people who are defining, creating, and building their story through the acquisition and application of products and services. Ideally they are or will become people who interact and transact with your company in meaningful and immersive ways, so that your brand can become part of each person's story.

When defining your *desired brand story participants* (aka consumers), keep it meaningful and relevant to your challenge. Avoid superfluous segmentation labels that relate to some proprietary study or trend book. Consumer analysis and research are valuable and encouraged, but be mindful of language and labels that make it difficult for everyone to understand who your consumers are and what they are like. Storyscaping is a team sport, so bringing everyone into the same understanding of your consumer is important. Anything or anyone who gets in the way of that goal can create an adverse effect. Make Storyscaping relevant to everyone you work with. You want people throughout your whole company and your extended company (your partners and your vendors) to own and share in the creation of stories and experiences for your brand; therefore, making it accessible and relevant is key.

Assuming you have identified the need for Storyscaping within your own organization, now it's important to understand the perspective upon which it is based, the terms and definitions that apply, and the foundations of the development model.

**No Void in the Experience Space.** One of the biggest impacts technology has produced on consumer-brand relationships is the proliferation of and simultaneous convergence of opportunities to engage and connect. We can no longer think about this solely from a media channel and distribution channel perspective.

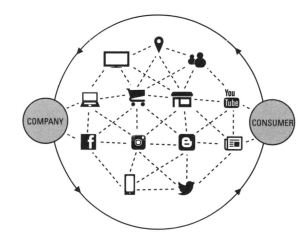

The potential experience space—the places and spaces where consumers and brands can engage in Purposeful connection—has become vastly extended and expanded by technology and so have the behaviors that technology enables. The Experience Space includes content generation and sharing, mobile commerce, applications, experiences that demonstrate brand utility (some kind of usefulness or functionality—a tool or a service), experiences that benefit the consumer, a media system, a social platform, or a physical space. Consider the Experience Space as the context in which the brand can better understand and service consumer needs, thereby creating a useful and Purposeful role for the brand in consumers' lives. Doing so provides both emotional value and experience value. Think of it as the space in which you will create a world for immersive experiences.

One of the first things to do is map out the potential Experience Space. This will help you understand the full context and opportunities for connection between your brand and the desired consumer. We explore how to more deeply understand the Experience Space even further in the following chapters.

**A Clear Perspective.** Now let's take our new appreciation for the Experience Space and look at how the brand and consumer connect across and through it. Let's park the complexity of the Experience Space in the background while we dive into the foundations of connection in a structured and logical way. We have already shared some examples around experience and story, so now let's look at how this maps out across the Experience Space.

To connect with consumers, the first thing a company must do is to stop referring to itself as a company and start thinking if itself as a brand. In its most simple (and we mean simple) terms, this is done with a form of personification. Why personification? When taking a very functional establishment (a company) and connecting it with consumers who are not always rational, a personification helps that company become more personable, even likeable to the consumer.

Once the personification is crafted as a brand, that brand is then applied to the products or services the company provides or creates. These products and services all serve a functional need. They provide a utility in some way, shape, or form.

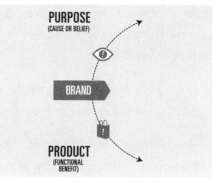

Typically, we try to find some form of product or service differentiation—a unique selling proposition (USP) is what we all learned in Marketing 101.

Today, the smarter companies have discovered and now operate based on a Brand Purpose, the brand's cause or belief.

Now shift to the other side of the Experience Space, where we consider the consumer. Consumers have functional and rational needs, such as to have clean clothes. These functional needs exist constantly and drive behavior.

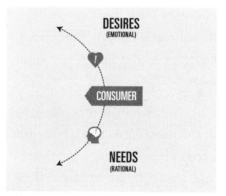

Consumers also have emotions, and emotional needs or desires, such as to be viewed as a good mom. The satisfaction of these desires makes the consumer feel good or better. In reality, these are inextricably linked. However, for the purpose of exploring the dimensions of consumer needs and how their story of self is defined by how and why they use certain things in their life, we look at consumers from both angles, the emotional and behavioral.

This is all rather straight-forward, and understanding these shared connections is key to the foundation of Storyscaping.

When a brand thinks, acts, and shares from its Purpose, it will connect with the consumer's emotional desires through the establishment of shared values.

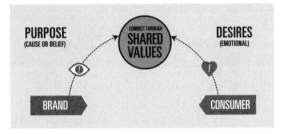

This is not the company toting, "We have these values," but rather transpires when the consumer emotionally connects with the same beliefs and values that the company displays when it delivers on its Purpose. Remember the TOMS Shoes example? It's a good example of the difference in impact this shift in perspective and behavior provides.[1]

Across the other dimension, at the most basic level, functional needs are solved with products and services that represent the means by which consumers define their own story. This connection

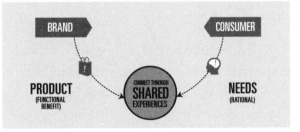

between a thing or form of utility and a person doing something creates a shared experience. Simply put, if there is a behavior, there is an experience.

As we have discussed earlier, some brands are great at connecting emotionally with story, whereas others deliver great products and build environments and things for great experiences. Our goal is to create a world for both, where shared stories exist as a Storyscape. Working from this understanding has unlocked much of our approach to Storyscaping and enabled our teams to effectively drive increased value on every dimension.

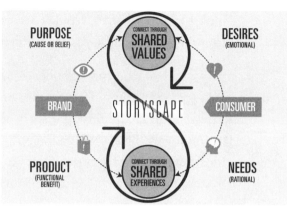

**Good Things Are Worth Evolving.** Much of this logic and theory isn't necessarily new. We took what made sense and evolved it with today's world in mind. Now, we have codified it into an operating model, thereby making this material more accessible to everyone. As part of the model, we introduce two new and key applications: the Organizing Idea and Systems Thinking as applied to stories and technology.

Our Storyscaping model is based on the concepts we just detailed, the perspective of connection and the understanding of Experience Space. Now that you have a basic understanding of where this journey leads, we will explore in greater detail each of the strategic pillars and elements mentioned in this chapter.

Through the next four chapters what we call the four pillars to an Organizing Idea will be explained and illustrated with examples, tips, and approaches. Then we'll take you on a deep dive into Organizing Ideas and provide tips on what to look for and what to avoid. This stabilizes your Storyscaping attempt with a good foundation around Organizing Ideas.

Then, the "new applications" section in the Storyscaping model come into play as we explore how you bring an Organizing Idea together with Systems Thinking to create the right story, Experience Space, connections, and enabling technologies. This is where the power of Storyscaping is realized—in an Organizing Idea, established from the pillars of understanding, which inform a Story System and ultimately create a world of immersive experiences (your very own Storyscape).

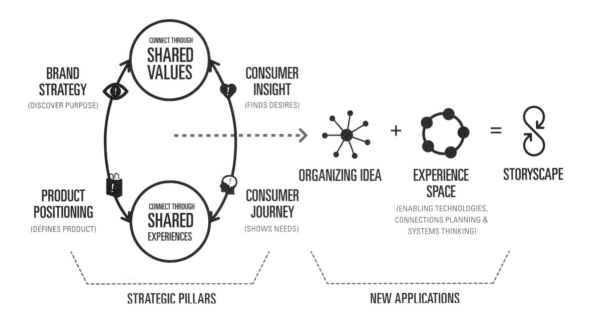

Given this model is not linear, you can start anywhere as long as you have an informed Organizing Idea and you apply it to an Experience Space. Equally so, at any one point in time, you may need to redevelop or create one aspect of the Story System (such as a new website). The model and principles still remain in effect, because the application of the model ensures that your creation is part of the larger system and is connected through the existing Organizing Idea.

# POWER OF WHY

*Unlocking Your Organization's Purpose
for Increased Brand Value*

# POWER OF WHY

*Unlocking Your Organization's Purpose*
*for Increased Brand Value*

What is the common denominator across the 50 brands showing the fastest growth, both in depth of customer relationships and financial value, between 2000 and 2010? That was a question posed by Karlene Lukovitz in a MediaPost article on January 18, 2012, referencing a study by Millward Brown and Jim Stengel.[1] The answer? "All of them, regardless of size or category, have been built on *an ideal* of improving lives in some way." That ideal is what we call Brand Purpose. It's a cause or a belief that the organization subscribes to, believes in, and exemplifies. It's the Purpose from which the brand should think, act, and share. This Purpose is the foundation under your entire enterprise, and it answers the question, "Why?" Why are you doing what you are doing? There is such a grand power behind why, and it has to be much greater, vaster, and wider scoped than merely earning profits. Remember, people's Spidey sense throws up the red flag on that! Foundationally speaking, we cannot stress enough the power of why and being right with yourself and your organization first. Everything, and we mean everything, ripples out from there, even the unseen.

The most successful and most enduring companies convey one clear and simple story through every action they take, not solely through their marketing. These companies believe in something much more aspirational than simply making money, and they behave accordingly. These companies know what they stand for; everything they do is informed by their Purpose, and everything they say follows—in that order. A recent summation from advertising industry leader Dan Wieden supports this: "The kind of brand that can thrive, is a brand that can tell a very simple and clear and coherent story about who they are, where they come from, who they work with and what they intend to do." The best of these companies learned to deliver their narrative through the products they make, the experiences they create, the services they provide, and even in the way they treat their employees and the communities they affect, not just in the way they communicate.

**Erect Pillars for Strength.** In Storyscaping, Purpose is the key pillar and the first of the four pillars. We consider each pillar as a support structure that serves critical characteristics for consumer connection, and this one is established through brand strategy. That strategy is also derived from consumer insight. As such, it should never be defined in isolation. Brand Purpose also serves as a guiding principal for the Organizing Idea. The Organizing Idea is key to making Storyscaping powerful. It connects the Story System, enabling a world of engagement and experience that every brand desires for heightened success, all of which will be explored in the following chapters.

There are plenty of books that tell great stories about Brand Purpose, for example, Joey Reiman's *The Story of Purpose*[2] or Simon Sinek's *Start with Why*,[3] and much of our thinking is inspired by them. Our goal here is to evolve that thinking for application in Storyscaping. We will explore how valuable it is and explain why it's important for context while we dig into the role of brand strategy to discover Brand Purpose, the dimensions of Purpose, and how it relates to Storyscaping.

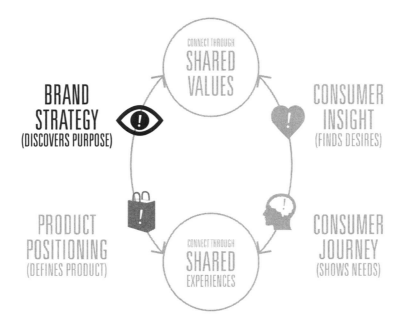

We believe that Purpose-driven organizations and brands are more inspiring for employees, stakeholders, and customers. True Purpose comes from within. Therefore, our approach is always one of discovery, not invention. Your statement of Purpose, cause, or belief needs to be the driving motivation for action. It should create relevance and meaning in everything your organization does and all that your brand represents. That is no small task. What does your Purpose sound like or look like? Do you already have a Purpose, or do you still need to define one? If you have one, is it appreciated universally, articulated well, and applied effectively? Let's look at what we define as the characteristics that make Purpose important.

**What Purpose Is Not.** Brand Purpose is vastly different to a company vision. A vision, although useful for setting goals and targets, has a limitation; you can see only so far into the future. A vision is about defining where a business wants to be. At the same time, your vision should be able to shift with the maturity of your business successes, failures, environmental influences, and so on. It should serve to guide a path, whereas a Purpose should be more timeless, more ethereal (in a good way). A Purpose is not a goal. Goals are what you want to achieve. Goals change over time as they are achieved or modified. Brand Purpose is not a strategy. Strategies are how you're going to get to your vision and achieve your goals. Your strategy today needs to offer more avenues, be more flexible and more dynamic than ever. Strategies employ tactics, which are also changing often. A Purpose is different from all of these defining elements of business and brand planning.

**What Purpose Is.** Purpose is emotive. It should be emotive for the people within the organization and also include an emotional dimension to how your brand behaves. As described earlier in the MediaPost article, it's about an "ideal of improving lives"—that is emotive. The U.S. Coast Guard Rescue Swimmers have a Purpose, "So others may live."[4] Some call it a motto; some call it a rally cry—we call it an emotive Purpose. It embodies the spirit of the rescue swimmers. It's critical to their belief and spirit, which enables them to do their jobs in the face of personal risk, adversity, and suffering. After all, a person doesn't just jump from a helicopter into a raging surf to rescue someone because upon awakening that morning he or she thought it was a good idea. Rescue swimmers do it because they believe in something bigger; they have a cause, and they personally connect with that cause in an emotional way, which inspires them to take action. For the highly trained and amazingly dedicated rescue swimmers, this Purpose is powerful.[5] It isn't a marketing line, tagline, or slogan for an ad. It's their *why*—why they do what they do, not how they do it or what results they hope to gain from doing it. It's not even an offer of service. And that's why Purpose is very different to marketing expressions. It should be the primary underpinning belief, a pillar of your foundation. The U.S. Coast Guard's motto and positioning as an entire organization is, "Semper Paratus" (always ready). This motto embodies their spirit (why), and in this case, it also works as a tagline and statement that positions how they serve. If you ever need the help of the Coast Guard, knowing that they are "always ready" provides a comforting and secure feeling. Can you see how this motto is emotional and personal and how "always ready" also has external consumer relevance as a positioning statement? Purpose doesn't always translate to a consumer expression ("So others may live"), but sometimes it just might (Coast Guard as a whole with the positioning tagline "always ready"). Now, stop and think about that for a second. Why do you get out of bed and go to work in the morning? Now, remove all the rational responses you just thought of and dig deeper to pinpoint your emotional connection. Why are you going to work? Hopefully you have a Purpose, one that inspires you and also connects with your brand.

Purpose should also be very simple. Walt Disney founded the entertainment empire with a simple statement: "To make people happy."[6] As part of the Disney team, this Purpose is inspiring and gives great focus on what they believe Disney is all about. You may also appreciate that this simple statement is rather generic. That's okay because Purpose isn't about differentiation. How you do things differentiates; why you do them does not. The ability of your Purpose to be universal and shared among the organization is critical. That's why simplicity and familiarity are key. What really counts is the defining of spirit and relevance to the company, culture, and how it inspires action.

When Sir Richard Branson, often considered a brand master in many respects, set up his first airline, Virgin Atlantic, he said, "I don't go into ventures to make a fortune. I do it because I'm not satisfied with the way others are doing business."[7] It's a simple and universally relevant premise. He wanted to create an airline he himself would enjoy flying on. His spirit was infused throughout all aspects of the new and growing airline. If you were a ground crew person or cabin crew person or pilot and you felt you were part of creating an airline that you would like to fly, you can imagine that amazing spirit alone would make the results better than average. The experience would be relevant every day. You would feel inspired to find things you could do to make the whole airline better. You certainly wouldn't throw guitars around the tarmac.

Having a clear Purpose enables everyone to think differently about the brand. It creates an emotional connection to the brand's existence beyond the rational reasons. Marc Pritchard, P&G's global marketing and brand-building officer, said, "Purpose certainly gets people to think about the brand differently, broadens their thinking about how the brand fits into their lives and is more relevant." The P&G brand Pampers is an example of this. Pampers' Purpose is "Baby's happy and healthy development."[8] Pampers' core product (diapers/nappies) serves a simple functional role: they keep the mess off the floor. They reverse gravity and catch the messy things babies do without warning or conscious consideration. They solve a simple need for clean floors (and other things of course). But, so do other diapers and nappies. How Pampers does it is different, as is their belief in why they are doing it. Pampers believes in "babies' happy, healthy development." As a brand, Pampers does everything it can to bring its Purpose to life—through products, content, experience, design, and much more. Pampers thinks about the baby, the mom, and the overall reasons why it does certain things, rather than just focusing on solutions to simple problems.

A statement of Purpose, cause, or belief is an internal platform that answers the question of why you exist. It's great when that Purpose serves some form of good for people and even better when it inspires emotional connections that are told through your brand narrative and brand experiences. Having a real and relevant Purpose as the foundation for your brand allows you to create shared values with consumers. This becomes the connection that motivates action. It creates relevance and meaning for employees and consumers because of the way it guides our actions, not because of its mere existence. It is the difference between inspiration (desire and loyalty) and manipulation (rational and functional satisfaction).

Unlocking, discovering, and defining your Purpose will give your brand new power—power to connect many stories and many experiences to an emotional platform. It must come from within the spirit and culture of the organization. Your history and foundation is always a good place to start, and don't settle on some historical premise if it lacks relevance. When working with clients to discover their Purpose, we involve as many of their people as we can, through many means, including storytelling. We also look deeply into the business to find emotional equity and its relevance to consumers. We seek real insight into how the brand improves people's lives. Don't settle on a nice, well-written line; strive for something real, inspiring, and relevant. Here's a real-world example. While working with a huge real estate development company to draw out their Purpose, we engaged a rigorous journey of discovery. Part of it entailed interviewing all of the board members, executives, and the chief executive officer (CEO), who by all accounts was a great leader. His role was critical to giving the Purpose credibility and value beyond the words themselves. He was also accountable for integrating the spirit and culture in a more pervasive way—a challenge he accepted. During his enlightening interview, we explained that the expectation was not for him to be amazed by what was defined; rather it was to be satisfied. When his response became "of course it's that," we knew it would be truly aligned to the organization. When this new powerful Purpose was presented at an executive meeting, he looked across the boardroom, smiled, and nodded with acknowledgment, comforted that what his entire company had created was true to the organization and was inspiring for their future. Since that day, they think, act, and share from their Purpose, "there is a better way to live."

**Applying Purpose with Purpose.** The application of Purpose is critical for effective Storyscaping. It defines the premise of the brand story, and it defines how the brand acts and what it does. We describe this as think, act, share. Let us explain that a bit. *Think* is about approaching everything from a perspective of Purpose. It is also *being* true to it. Ask yourself if you are in line with the belief or if you are solving for the cause. *Act* is about how you deliver, what you do, when you do it, and so on. It's about building great experiences. *Share* is part communication (saying it), part interaction (enabling), and part listening (dialogue). Sharing while being in line with your Purpose also means involving people in your Purpose. You have to be willing to lean into criticism and listen attentively. This creates participation with your brand instead of just sending people messages. It should be about the enablement of sharing and the act of sharing in content and in spirit. Beyond think, act, share, the order of your approach is also critical. We learned this from the leadership model shared by Simon Sinek.[9] In fact, we always say, "inspired by Simon Sinek," partly because that is what a Brand Purpose should do and partly because it's his Purpose to inspire others.

**This is the model we apply; it is based on the Golden Circles by Simon Sinek.**

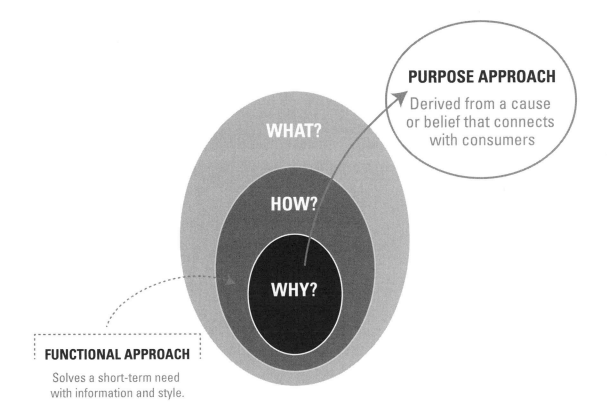

**PURPOSE APPROACH**
Derived from a cause or belief that connects with consumers

**FUNCTIONAL APPROACH**
Solves a short-term need with information and style.

## WHY

Purpose, cause, or belief, the driving motivation for action. It creates relevance and meaning. Connected with a consumer insight for Brand Purpose.

## HOW

Guiding principles. The specific actions that are taken to deliver your Purpose. The values by which you operate.

## WHAT

Proof, rational reasons. The tangible and rational ways in which you bring your Purpose to life.

Simon's Golden Circle Approach teaches us to always work from the middle out—start from your *why* (Purpose), move to the *how* (means), and finally address the *what* (things you produce or do). This is how leaders work and how great brands work like leaders. What do great leaders and great brands have in common? A clear, meaningful, and relevant Purpose. Yes, they always think, act, and share from the inside out (why, how, what). Another benefit they also share comes from what Purpose achieves—a form of inspired magnetism, earned because people share in the values expressed and desired.

**The Journey of Discovery, Not Invention.** When working to discover your Purpose, you may find it to be a natural extension of the reason you set up your business in the first place: what you wanted to do to improve the lives of others. This is a great foundation, and it is especially effective when you are just starting out or if you're running a small enterprise. When you become well established, the journey is a little more complex, as is the case if you are a large enterprise with many people. Either way, your goal is to be clear and inspiring so that the Purpose can serve as an effective foundation throughout the organization, be that 10 people or 10,000 people.

The way you go about discovering your organization's Purpose can vary according to the type of business and the nature of brands. Is your brand a product brand or an organization brand? If you are an organization brand, your journey of discovery looks more deeply into the spirit and culture of your people. If you are a product brand, like a consumer packaged goods (CPG) brand, you will need to look more deeply into consumer relevance and consumer desires. Recognizing these differences, we will share the elements of discovery and approach we use. And, as you explore your Purpose, you may lean into these with more or less detail as is appropriate. One thing remains universal: the spirit of discovery, rather than invention. Don't just make something up. Either think deeply into your real Purpose if you are a sole trader or take the time and effort to dig into business and brand, allowing these to inform what you define as your Brand Purpose.

The approach is to establish the consumer connection and relevance through insight while establishing and defining the why, how, and what as discussed previously.

**The process we follow has four steps**

| IMMERSE | ASSESS | ORIGINATE | ARTICULATE |
|---|---|---|---|
| History Audit | Leadership Interviews | Purpose Workshop | Brand Blueprints |
| Social Audit | | | Brand Strategy Presentations |
| Consumer & Category Research | Research Analysis | | Internal Comms Programs |
| Employee Workshops | Strategic Distillation | Strategy Creation | Research Validation |
| Employee Research | | | |

Process for establishing consumer connection.

First, *Immerse*: This stage is about digging into the history and spirit of the organization. The goal here is to understand the foundation of the organization and how that has manifested over time. Additionally, through the use of research, we also seek to understand the consumer to ensure relevance. During the last part of this step, we interact with employees through both direct interaction and research in efforts to understand how they witness the brand improving people's lives. Having them tell stories of the past and provide thoughts and feelings based on potential scenarios can be a powerful means of unlocking insight into the reasons a brand exists, how it operates, and how it is relevant to consumers.

Second, *Assess*. Here we connect with and explore how organizational leadership sees the brand, the culture, and the future of the brand and business. These leaders are the most powerful influence on how a Purpose is extended among the people and through the actions of the business. As such, getting firsthand insight is critical. The analysis of research and strategic distillation is used to draw out insight and key learnings. We seek information about what has been said or done in the historical past that has defined the brand. What role has the brand played in people's lives over time? What values have been consistent through history? Additionally, we start to distill the learnings down to consumer insights so that we can establish areal platform for relevance. In doing this, we look for cultural insight, category insight, and emotionally relevant consumer insight. When analysing these insights, we describe them as

- The cultural influence lens: consumer trends that influence how we see things, how we behave relative to others, and how we want to be seen.
- The category/product interaction lens: how we engage with the category/products now, what we know, think, how we behave.
- The consumer insight lens: a revelation about human behavior or an emotion that can be leveraged.

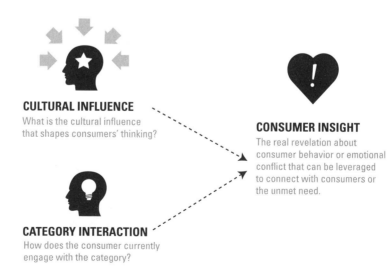

**CULTURAL INFLUENCE**
What is the cultural influence that shapes consumers' thinking?

**CATEGORY INTERACTION**
How does the consumer currently engage with the category?

**CONSUMER INSIGHT**
The real revelation about consumer behavior or emotional conflict that can be leveraged to connect with consumers or the unmet need.

This is drawn from category interaction and cultural influence. We look for the conflict or unmet needs and desires that are established between cultural influences and how we engage with the category.

In step three, *originate*, we apply this content to interactive sessions with a team of mixed organizational representatives. This is where final insights are defined, values are explored and articulated further, and expressions of Purpose are examined. The discussions and exercises are centred around the content drawn from the previous steps, sometimes in video stories, quotes, pictures, research data, and so on. Encourage these discussions to be immersive, expressive, engaging, honest, and spirited. Remember, your desired outcomes answer the *why, how,* and *what* as described earlier.

Last, we *articulate*. The outcomes are tightened and tested against the insights for relevance and expressed in their most inspiring way. Communication is determined by what is appropriate for the brand and organization. Strategies are articulated, and now with this coveted and customized information, the brand has a new foundation where it can establish emotional connections with consumers.

Of course, this is just the beginning of your discovery with Purpose. You may choose to leave this newly discovered Purpose as words and values, or maybe you will add some pictures and sounds, or you can take it to a higher level by applying it to how you think, act, and share. When you do, you create the opportunity to build powerful emotional connections with people through shared values. Creating shared values happens when a consumer believes in the same values that a brand portrays. How does a brand portray these values? By thinking, acting, and sharing based on their Purpose—a Purpose that is relevant to the consumer's emotional desires. In Storyscaping, we use consumer insights to draw out emotional desires so that the brand finds emotional relevance and can then truly connect with the consumer.

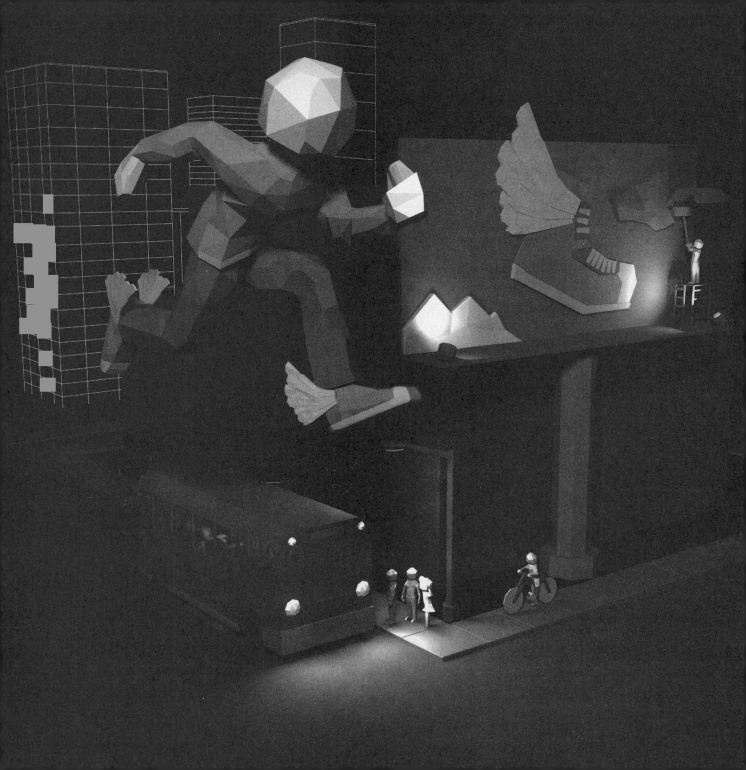

# WALK THE WALK

*Driving the Authentic Brand Behaviors*
*That Fuel Business Growth*

# WALK THE WALK

*Driving the Authentic Brand Behaviors
That Fuel Business Growth*

In the last chapter, we looked at Brand Purpose as the cause or belief of your organization, thereby highlighting the mega important answer as to *why* your organization exists and why people should care. Let's move forward with the process of successful Storyscaping by introducing the next pillar, it covers the *how* and *what*. Here we will uncover the means by which your organization satisfies consumer needs, the means by which you operate, the means by which you treat consumers, and the services or products you provide. These simple little words hold big power when you directly connect them. *How* you operate should always be based on and support your Purpose, in every way, shape, and form. *What* you offer as a product or service should be a real consequence of your Purpose (*why*) and *how* you create and deliver it. This is also demonstrated as the act and share behaviors of operating with a Purpose. Remember? "Think, act, and share" from your Purpose.

Actions speak louder than words; therefore, our actions—what we do and how we behave—contribute disproportionally to our brand perception. Our actions weigh in with much more value than our words do (what we say about ourselves). In fact, you can build an incredibly strong brand without ever doing an ounce of paid advertising. We don't recommend it, but it can certainly be done. Conversely, you can do a ton of great advertising, but if you have a crap product, provide a poor experience, or behave disingenuously, then your business is doomed. Every interaction with a brand, service, or product is an experience. You cannot separate them and always want to think of your brand positioning (how it delivers) with that experience in mind. The product or service is the functional offer that enables this experience to be what it is. The type of experience, how it meets your functional needs, how it relates to the brand story, and how it is all connected are critical to building a world of immersive experiences. To be effective with Storyscaping connected experiences, we have to understand the role of the brand and its positioning, how functional products and services enable experience, and how the positioning and product must align authentically to your Purpose. After that discussion, we will explore a logical approach to how we can position your product or service as the "gift," which will help define the Organizing Idea of your Storyscape.

**Positioning for Position.** Everyone has a story about being overwhelmed by choice. Try ordering a cup of coffee from choices micro-organized by phylum, class, order, family, genus, or species. A consumer today has to make a spectrum of choices before even stepping up to the counter: What size? Is it going to be coffee or a different specialty hot drink? If coffee, which roast?  Bold, low acid, mild, rich and lively? How much sweetener? What kind of sweetener? Dairy? Other alternatives? Just a coffee? What about a sweet treat during the coffee or mint for after?

*From the movie* **L.A. Story:**
**Tom:** I'll have a decaf coffee.
**Trudi:** I'll have a decaf espresso.
**Morris Frost:** I'll have a double decaf cappuccino.
**Ted:** Give me decaffeinated coffee ice cream.

**Harris:** I'll have a half double decaffeinated half-caf, with a twist of lemon.
**Trudi:** I'll have a twist of lemon.
**Tom:** I'll have a twist of lemon.
**Morris Frost:** I'll have a twist of lemon.
**Cynthia:** I'll have a twist of lemon.

This comedic exchange is more than two decades old, but it quite aptly illustrates the dilemma of many modern consumers today. In 1991 it was a hyperbolic exchange to illustrate the ridiculousness of many Los Angelenos' lives, but today, there is nothing exaggerated about it and it could go on twice as long when it comes to the options. In a world of choice, especially one that is amplified by the marketer's desire to meet expectations and personalize offerings, the ways in which a brand is positioned (its how) serves as signposts for navigation. This is achieved through the stories we attach to the symbols used by brands for signposting. These stories are either new to the customer and created by the brand, or they are customers' stories built on past experience and interaction with the brand and its products/services.

It's almost provincial how simple coffee ordering used to be and how commonplace ridiculousness has become in the consumer journey. Where there is so much choice in the marketplace, brands actually have a greater challenge because there is room for many more stories and, in today's mode, many more experiences. Our goal is, of course, to remove the risk that consumers will make choices based on a quick game of rock, paper, scissors and respond more emotionally, based on your brand and the stories and experiences that it conjures up. Brands are symbols and can be triggers for stories of the brand and the consumer's experience with that brand and its products. By reinforcing how a brand is positioned you will earn a direct effect on the story it tells and the experience it inspires.

The reality is, consumers are savvy. They are more informed about the very nature of buying—what to look for, where to research, and whom to ask when buying a product. The consequence? A vast array of content and information from which to construct these stories that all have their needs at the center. Remember, the customer is the hero. Which means the brand positioning needs to directly define the product or service as a gift that helps or enables the hero in some way. Beyond the functional aspects, effectively achieving this will enable the brand and product to play a meaningful role in the consumer's story, which can serve as a whopping big signpost from which to navigate.

**The Consequence of Expectation.** People no longer narrow-mindedly focus on just the brand name as they once did. They care more about their holistic *experiences* with the products and services as dimensions of the brand. The expectation of universal satisfaction has created a more empowered consumer stance. For example, if Molly thinks Bombshell Blonde really turned her hair Brassy Bimbo, she now has the ability to influence all her friends about it, with emotional words, photos, and/or video! With every bit the expertise reserved for TV pundits, your neighbor Molly can influence her entire neighborhood and beyond. Her social media friends and followers have the ability to promote her experience by simple clicks and shares, and before you know it Bombshell Blonde hits the bargain bin.

Constantly growing expectations among diverse audiences who are empowered to have what they want leads to a simple marketing directive, give the consumer what they desire; give them choice. The ability to satisfy a diverse audience who has high expectations is to offer choice. This is a marketing fundamental that was born out of consumer research, which tells us to establish what the consumer wants and then satisfy his or her needs. When we do this, the marketing outcome is greater range—the ability to target more specific consumer needs. The consumer outcome is choice, which satisfies the consumer's need. It all works together. In this mind space, we need to proceed with caution so that we do not create consumer bewilderment—*too much choice*—making it even more difficult to build a position for consumers to navigate. In fact, it can counter our goal of building a meaningful connection through shared experiences and shared values. A second pitfall is that you run the risk of providing more than what a consumer is willing to pay for or finds valuable—*too much entitlement*. That's why the additive value of story is so important. There is nothing wrong with having a range of products where it is relevant, as long as you ensure that your brand has a clear means for how it delivers. You need to have a clear and distinct brand story that consumers can build into their story. And as you expand your business, think long and hard about how that expansion will be based on your Purpose and connected to your brand story. By doing so, you can create choice without creating confusion or bewilderment.

**A Functional Solution to Experience Differentiation.** For decades, maybe even centuries, most marketing started with the product or service differentiator. *What is unique about our product or service? Knowing that, we can communicate it far and wide. With good creative, we will cut through the clutter and leverage the emotional value of our brand and then we won't be able to keep the shelves stocked.* Sound familiar? In simplistic terms, this, along with a good understanding of the 4 Ps, has served many businesses well. In fact, today plenty of businesses still tackle marketing this way, which sets things up pretty well for a while. However, that "while" may only be fleeting, and soon you may find it difficult to scale or increase margins. You may even form a drug-like dependency on advertising. Increased competition, mass distribution, and social network connection are all things that can put a dent in this simple approach fairly quickly, too. That said, in the same way we believe in retaining and leveraging the traditional knowledge of storytelling, we believe some of the fundamentals of classic marketing should still serve a role. It is the way we use them that needs a new approach.

One of the reasons some of the core principles remain effective is simply because consumers still have functional needs. That's a simple fact—a fact that we can't ignore and could instead leverage in our creation of powerful and meaningful shared experiences. A shared experience is derived from a need being satisfied or solved by a product or service that a company provides. The interaction itself creates the shared experience. Through Storyscaping, our goal is to create worlds where immersive experiences are shared between brand and consumer in several ways. This is why it is so important to understand and leverage the value of products/services and their delivery—so that we can truly maximize these experiences. Doing this, while keeping in line with the Brand Purpose, helps support the bridge to emotional connection, because you can't separate emotional from functional in real terms. If a product fails or is delivered in a substandard way, the positive emotion a consumer has for a brand becomes bruised. An honest mistake may get a pass once, maybe even twice, but eventually, poor performance of any kind will destroy the connection and will also create a negative consumer out of your potential ambassador. And it certainly does not build new customers to replace the lost ones. Imagine dining with some friends in a new restaurant. This restaurant received rave reviews from food critics. It has a cool website that books reservations by table location and is promoted on UrbanDaddy e-mails.[1] Your expectations are high, and anticipation is palpable. You arrive. The décor isn't really your style, but it's appropriate; the ambience is fine, and the food is great. However, the waiter is a little arrogant, and you feel it every time you ask for something. He does the job, asks the right questions, and doesn't drop your food—he delivers. Yet, you still feel an energy that puts you on edge, not allowing you to fully immerse yourself into the experience. You exit with that underthrilled feeling. This new restaurant missed the mark; it was not a great dinner. Your real-life experience did not match the emotional connection you had built before arriving.

We have all had this sort of experience, and most likely, if someone were to ask you for your opinion on this restaurant, you would probably say the food was good and the service was crap, even though you may not be able to rationalize why in fine detail; you just don't feel right recommending it. You don't really want it to become part of your world. You feel disappointed and disconnected from how you felt—your emotional connection—in the beginning based on the restaurant's communication and online experience. The point is, that although the product (food and environment) and the marketing experience (communication and website) were good, even great, other factors contributed to the experience. A crack in that experience can sever the emotional connection. As such, we need to always think of products and services as enablers for an experience. They must remain connected throughout the Experience Space bound to all other channels, such as digital interactions and social conversations.

We often are asked to consult on helping chief marketing officers reshape their marketing departments. The common questions tend to be mostly about organizational design or "tell us what kind of people and skills we should hire," and so on. We often uncover that the issue does not lie in lack of skills; often it's the team's perspective that is broken. We point to the travel and hospitality industry as a better (not perfect) model because these organizations often guide themselves with the compass of guest experience. This is an effective perspective, which puts the customer clearly in the heart of the story and drives a ton of good organizational behaviors. Although a lot of marketing investment and focus zeros in on building emotional connection, we believe that getting the functional side (especially the service side) of the house in line is also critical. To do that, we need to consider even a functional solution as an experience enabler. In fact, that is the foundation of the experience because consumers always seek to solve a need. Meeting their need with a solution is the very basis for a shared experience. And we know that telling a brand story without an experience is only one-third of the equation.

Beyond the service world of restaurants, the same applies in our relationship with everyday needs and products. We wake up every morning, and whether we are conscious of it or not, we need to breathe. It's a simple biological need—inhaling a breath of air with around 21 percent oxygen.[2] It's so functional that it's purely instinctive. Imperative as this oxygen is, unless you're deprived of it, the act of breathing isn't very emotional; therefore, you probably wouldn't consider it an experience. But look again. A need (to breathe) is being solved by a product (air), with an action or behavior (inhaling), which enables a positive experience (life).

From there, we evolve our functional needs. It might be to have clean teeth (for simplicity, the following assumptions are based on a male). So, we head off to the bathroom and are confronted by the toothpaste, toothbrush, soaps, moisturizers, shave cream, deodorant, mouthwash, aftershave, razor blades, sunscreen, hair product, brush/comb, and so on. All these are within steps of our slumber. Each product shapes, forms, or satisfies a need we have—fresh breath or tamed hair. It's all working to satisfy a need (functional and emotional). How we interact with each of these products and the brands they embody is an experience in and of itself. A behavior occurs, we use the product, we have an experience of how it delivers, how it feels, how it smells, how it looks, and so on, all of which connect us to how we feel about that product, the brand, and ourselves. Although it may seem dramatized here, it all counts when you're building a brand and growing a business. We can no longer think of products from just a design perspective; we should look deeply from the experience perspective. Doing so will unlock a new dimension for product differentiation in a very competitive landscape.

The beauty and personal care space alone, which includes those products that are "needs" surrounding your first step of the day, makes up approximately $68 billion in the United States. From a marketing investment perspective, brands spent around $6.8 billion on advertising.[3] Multiply that across the globe, and that's some significant investment. And those dollars do not include what is used to enable physical experiences (from websites to product form), which, in our view should be a lot. With keen focus on the experience, we can see that every aspect of interaction with these products is part of the experience. How the products are developed, packaged, sold, distributed, and supported all matters. Why? They solve for a need; there is great importance on how the products taste, feel, look, work; and so on. Functional characteristics contribute to how we experience a product. At the same time, this (like the restaurant example) is also framed based on your expectations and connection to the category and brand, which are often established through communication and other brand interactions. For example, if a product has a faulty closure and the consumer calls customer service about it, the way he or she is treated during that communication also counts toward or against the product and experience with the brand. Where you buy these products is relevant, too. "Are they at my regular store, in stock, in my preferred flavor?" All this is functional, so the functional reality of marketing remains true. It remains a core characteristic of product and service delivery. The way we leverage this as part of an immersive experience within the brand world equals the new opportunity. Aligning the product or service, the offer, the distribution, and so on, to the Brand Purpose constitutes how we deliver, and it is critical to success.

**Walking the Walk.** How your business performs its every day tasks, how it treats people, and how your products solve everyday needs are paramount when delivering on your Purpose. This is the way brands and companies build the connection beyond functional solutions, even though the service or product provides a functional solution as described earlier. The relevance and effect of how you act actually builds the shared experience. This is why, in our hyperconnected world, where consumers have amazing power, you have to walk the walk, not just talk the talk. You have to be true to your Purpose. You have to be authentic, and you have to be transparent. Masking reality by blasting overstated marketing messages through mass communication no longer works. If you look at the way many great brands have grown, you will see they are very authentic in their approach, their actions, their behaviors, and the experiences they create.

**Transparency Is Fashionable.** "Transparency, inside and out. Too much focus is on what is being said by a brand versus what a brand/company actually does—brands need authenticity," Dame Vivienne Westwood, fashion designer and activist, smartly stated. Dame Westwood is an icon in her own right and is renowned for many things, including the success and longevity of her fashion brand. From the days of punk rock to now, her brand has challenged the world with honesty and a forthright expression of her perspectives. This authenticity has been a cornerstone of her brand, as have the experiences she creates through her designs, not to mention the experiences created because of them[4]. We have had various discussions with Dame Westwood; we studied her brand, her activism, and her work, and each provided insight into how stories can create movements—through authenticity—over a long period of time. The mere fact that Dame Westwood continues her success well beyond her origin in the punk movement is a testament to being flexible and staying relevant. Additionally, her story succeeds in a time of great innovation that has changed much of the way we connect, communicate, share, and tell stories. Her story truly reflects the power of the same and highlights the importance of transparency and authenticity, no matter the cause or Purpose: "When I design clothes I have to like them and the clothes have always got a story, but you put those clothes on different people, that is, people wear them, and that story becomes part of their personal story as well." Dame Westwood also shares the story of when Paloma Picasso was thanking Yves Saint Laurent for his designs just before he passed away. "She said thank you Yves, for making me more Spanish, more 40 years old, more Paloma, more dramatic. . . . what she was saying was, you gave me myself and all the facets of me that I discovered through wearing your clothes."

These are stories for how design can be created by using authenticity as a core foundation. These authentically formulated designs create experiences for the wearer, which ultimately become part of the wearer's story. So, although not all brands are from Yves Saint Laurent or Vivienne Westwood, they exemplify the value of being authentic to your Purpose and how it serves more meaningful connections and experiences with your consumer.

Authenticity alone does not engender an experience. It should define the relationship between Brand Purpose and experience, but it will not create a movement. A movement requires inspiration and experience. The key to driving authenticity is a universal and constant commitment to your Purpose. When you waver from your cause and belief, you will typically lose connection with what is real to your spirit and culture. Great leaders in all levels of business (not just chief executive officers) are easily recognized as those who are rich in the culture of the brand and true to its Purpose. Think about whom in your organization exemplifies this. In what ways can you further engender authenticity and Purpose into how you act every day and what you produce or do for people through your products and services?

Being able to achieve this for a service, a product, or a combination (service product) of these demands that you truly understand the expectations of consumers. Before we get to that (we discuss the needs and desires of consumers in Chapters 7 and 8), and with the understanding that product and service function in authentic Purpose-driven ways in order to create experiences, we can now explore how we position the brand and product/service as a pillar for an Organizing Idea.

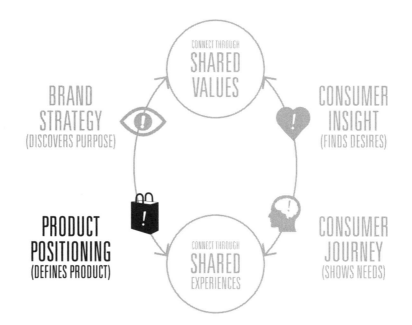

**The Gift of Function.** As we discussed earlier, there are long-term benefits earned from story and experience differentiation. To achieve this, we believe that your brand needs an Organizing Idea, an idea that helps inspire the type of experiences you have through the brand's Storyscape. How the product or service is positioned represents one of the pillars for the Organizing Idea. The job of the Organizing Idea is to organize experiences that relate to how your product or service is positioned. This ensures relevance and connection to the functional consumer needs that it solves, therefore bringing to life the shared experiences that enable participation in the brand story.

Over the years, many models and approaches have aimed to define positioning: single-minded propositions (SMPs), value statements, the 5 Ws & H approach, brand essence, brand archetype, and so on. Each can provide value and play a part based on your preferences, beliefs, approaches, and needs. In fact, if you are looking to gain funding for a start-up, a value proposition is essential. However, if you are building a world or creating an experience, these won't help. Here we need to evolve and push forward to the experience dimension that connects to the brand story through an Organizing Idea. We believe this new dimension is more relevant to the positioning for shared experiences and Organizing Ideas. Remember, you define your product or service in terms of its role as the gift, allowing your brand to play the role of mentor and enabling the consumer to connect with the experience and story as the hero.

**Step Up Your Walk.** Let's break that down one more layer as it relates to our Storyscaping approach. First, our hero has emotional desires and thus is on a quest for satisfaction of those desires. The brand, through its Purpose (belief and cause), aligns itself, like a good mentor does, to the hero's desire, thereby emotionally supporting and encouraging the hero's quest. This creates a sharing of values between hero and mentor. Look alive. This quest isn't fictional; it's real. The hero travels a path of behaviors to solve his or her quest. Along that path the mentor helps the hero by providing a magical gift (product or service) that satisfies the hero's desires and creates a shared journey (experience). The plot of this tale is written directly from the Organizing Idea.

Here's a fun exercise to bring these concepts closer to home. Complete the following story line using your organization:

On the hero's journey to satisfy _____
[insert consumer need], we, as the mentor, provide a gift of
_____ [insert product / service] that magically
_____ [insert offer, single-minded differentiator, value
proposition], thereby creating a journey that _____
(describe experience benefit).

Let's explore a few ways this could look:

On the hero's journey to *become a fit and healthier person,* we, as the mentor, provide a gift of *the new fuel band wearable activity monitor* that magically *enables them to monitor and share their daily activity,* thereby creating a journey that *inspires shared participation in increased physical activity*.

On the hero's journey to *fight boredom,* we, as the mentor, provide a gift of *Vitaminwater* that magically *makes boring brilliant,* thereby creating a journey that *makes you part of a less boring world*.

On the hero's journey to *zip around town,* we, as the mentor, provide a gift of *the Fiat 500* that magically *gives you style inside and out*, thereby creating a journey that *elevates your "presence," not your car size*.

Based on this logic, you can define the positioning and role of product as a pillar for the Organizing Idea. It will, in turn, inform the Story System and shape your Storyscape. And remember, this must be in relation to your understanding of the consumer for relevance and meaning.

# INSIGHT TO DESIRE

*Understanding the Values
and Aspirations of the Consumer*

# INSIGHT TO DESIRE

*Understanding the Values and Aspirations
of the Consumer*

Have you ever observed the intriguing phenomenon where dogs and their owners have similar looks, personalities, or traits? Do you think that is something people rationally strive for or just a natural occurrence resulting from the deep-seated love for their dogs? Our devotion to our dogs is often well beyond rational, much the same way they love us unconditionally and beyond reason. The joyous pants and tail wags we are greeted with upon our return home every day—not just on the good days; the compassionate look pulsing from those big brown eyes when we confide in them with our deepest thoughts. How about the smile they give when we bring out their favorite toy? All these interactions make us feel great and the mutuality is palpable. It's all related to the emotional connection we have with them. Even if the dog cannot actually smile at us, we feel a smile because we feel connected beyond the rational or logical, and we appreciate the slightest recognition of that (even if it's only our imagination).

Have you ever wondered why it's so difficult to express what it means to be in love? Love is believed to be one of the most emotional feelings we have. The feeling of love comes from the deepest emotional triggers in our brains (sorry, it's not our hearts). Scientists have studied the brain for many years to understand the differences between emotional and rational thinking. It is regularly suggested that there are different parts inside our complex and brilliant brains, where emotion and logic live. It has also been suggested that things such as language and expression, which are learned skills, activate a different part of the brain than emotions and feelings. Then it stands to reason that logic is easier to explain than an emotion such as love. This bit of knowledge counters the clichéd gender difference that men find it more difficult to express feelings; instead, it's more to do with mere physiology. Working from this premise of language as logic and love as emotion, it makes perfect sense why it's much harder to express what love is.

These are just a couple of examples to illustrate that not every decision is simple or logical. Logic will not drive emotions, and emotions have as much to do with behavior as logic does. Emotions without the logic to guide the behavior simply stimulates feelings. This is the reason we need to explore both rational needs and emotional desires when we are looking to connect brands with consumers across the Experience Space.

In this chapter, we are specifically looking at consumer insights into emotional influences and desires. We will dig into what we should look for and provide some ideas on how to think about consumer insights. We value and appreciate that communities of marketers, psychologists, sociologists, researchers, and others have all spent years studying the consumer and offer great insight, methods, and understandings. We will touch on some of these concepts and teachings as they apply to Storyscaping and use them to add context in an honest, yet by design, superficial way. But instead of exploring the depths of "the collective unconscious," the "principles of socialization," or similar concepts, our aim is to build understanding and application as it relates to Storyscaping.

**Change or Cash In.** No one would argue with the statement that we live in a world of change. Some argue that the rate of change with modern technology is faster than ever. The reality is that everything is faster, bigger, better, and smarter than it was before—even our phones are smart now. That's called evolution, and every generation sees some form of it. That's why no matter what generation you are from—Baby Boomer, Gen Y, Gen X, Gen C, Gen Z, Gen Alphabet—you will at some stage utter, "When I was young. . . ." Simply put, change is inevitable. General Eric Shinseki, former U.S. Army Chief of Staff, stated, "If you don't like change, you're going to like irrelevance even less."[1] Although his comment was in reference to adapting within the armed forces, it also works well with respect to how our social connectedness and networked lives have created a heightened need to keep up with change. The expectation is on us as much as it is on the social manifestation of a world enabled by ubiquitous technology. The ways in which we interact, connect, share our lives, and tell our stories have all changed with the influence of our always-on technology that we just can't live without. At the same time, the power of using stories to engage and connect us emotionally hasn't changed. Why not? Because even though our world is changing, the underlying psychology of how we respond emotionally hasn't changed. Maslow's hierarchy of needs is as relevant today as it ever was. What about Jung's theories about archetypes and the collective unconscious? Yes, also still relevant. Even a peek at a more recent perspective, like that of Hugh Mackay (in his book *What Makes Us Tick? The Ten Desires That Drive Us*), proves that the old theories are still in good working order.[2] A healthy understanding of these theories and concepts related to our psychological desires is helpful. It's also important to remember that people are people. Although we are each different, we are complicated, we are imperfect, we live in a world of change, we also have very common and connected emotional desires. These are the very desires that we can leverage for brand stories and brand connections—magical ones that enable shared values and provide great consumer insights.

**Skin in the Game.** To find, discover, rediscover, or unearth great insights, we need more than context and an appreciation for emotional desires; we need to step into the skin of our consumers. Wherever possible, we strongly suggest enlisting deep and broad research behind insights appropriate for the challenge. At SapientNitro, we are blessed with a powerful team of researchers and insight specialists who provide rich understanding and input into our thinking. We strongly believe in the power of research and highly recommend each and every application of the Storyscaping model be built around the knowledge drawn from real consumer understanding—no matter how that is established.

Our goal here is to connect our brands and consumers on an emotional level using shared values, stories, and experiences in an effort to inspire consumer participation. To claim success, we really need to understand the consumer; the influences on their emotions; how they feel about things; and how our brands, stories, and experiences can remain relevant in the hyperconnected, always-on world. This requires real insight—not just observation but an inside, personal scoop.

Insight is a broad word and is often overused, even abused, among our marketing brethren. Our industry includes people who are "insight specialists" and are part of "insight teams." To us, what these folks represent is a desire to understand consumers. The Merriam-Webster Dictionary defines *insight* as "the ability to understand people and situations in a very clear way," going on to describe it as "the act or result of apprehending the inner nature of things or of seeing intuitively." It means that in order to have great consumer insight, we really need to explore the inner nature of why people do the things they do and how they feel about those things. At the same time, intuition and Spidey sense play a role in defining great insight too. It's a simple fact that although research is scientific, mathematical, and typically involves technology, people are people—imperfect and sometimes irrational. Therefore intuition, experience, and diverse understanding all play role in exploring consumer insight.

When it comes to brands, we often consider consumer insight as being "a revelation about human behavior or an emotion that can be leveraged to connect a brand" or "a new usable perspective on the relationship between a brand and its existing or intended consumers." Insights are sometimes discovered as widely recognized truths or habits. Alternatively, insights may come from grasping or comprehending the obscurity of things. In other words, they might not be obvious or intuitive at first, but insights should always exude truth in their discovery.

In Storyscaping, one of the four pillars for an Organizing Idea is consumer insight. When working on this pillar, we sort and find one paramount insight that will connect the brand and consumers on an emotional level, in a relevant way, and in a manner that inspires creativity to fuel the brand story. We look for the strongest and most motivating insight we can leverage. Brilliant brand stories are created from brilliant insights. This particular insight into consumers' emotions and feelings is likely to identify a challenge that the brand can solve for the consumer. It is a reflection of the consumer's everyday experience, attitudes, views, or values. It's a critical component for creating a meaningful brand connection and for creating a Storyscape that connects with consumers. Spare no effort to understand consumers and earn this insight. Collaborate with others and explore options and opportunities. Also apply your Spidey sense because intuition is a powerful tool, especially when it comes to insight.

As we continue along the journey of Storyscaping, we look for and identify many other insights from different perspectives or lenses. In Chapter 6, we briefly looked at cultural insights and category insights. Additional exploration of consumer behaviors and their interactions with products, distribution, transactions, media, content, and each of these in social media must happen.

**Fancy Meeting You Here.** The first step to great insight is having a very clear view of consumers. The tighter and more specific your consumer definition is the more focused your insight can be. Conversely, if you have a broad consumer group, your insights will most likely be very broad. For example, let's say you are promoting a tourism destination and your potential participants are located all over the globe. For you, consumer insight is likely to be very high level and include a limited and common emotional understanding across people from many markets, many cultures, and many environments. Yet, if you are looking at teens in their last year of high school, you can be very specific with your focus. Both instances are perfectly acceptable because they are based on your consumer brand connection challenge. The key is to have it defined. When you do, you will be better equipped to explore insights within the frame defined by the desired group.

Truly understanding the emotional toils or cultural influences of a consumer is priceless. No amount of effort, exploration, or discovery is too much when it comes to finding fresh and authentic insight. It pays to explore all the dimensions of consumers and their emotional variances. When we look at a typical consumer as illustrated, we explore insights at every stage. In doing so, we ensure that our exploration delves into dimensions of cultural influence and competitive influence. We are looking for new and usable perspectives on consumer emotion and desires. Let's unpack that a little further.

**Ask and You Shall Receive.** We start with the human need or stimulus. In this illustration we explore "thirst"—an unconscious feeling that triggers a need. We can explore the reasons we get thirsty by asking appropriate questions: Is it a time of day occurrence? Is it environmental? Is it health? Is it instinctive, like breathing? When thirsty, how do we feel and why do we feel that way? So many questions to ask and answer, and we are only at step 1!

The category of drinks is huge, so on with more questions: What do we already know about drinks? What don't we know? What have we had in the past? What influences us? What are the trends? Why do we like one drink over another? What is the competitive landscape? Why are there so many choices? How do we navigate choice? How do we feel about the category and why? This step includes a lot of discovery around the category.

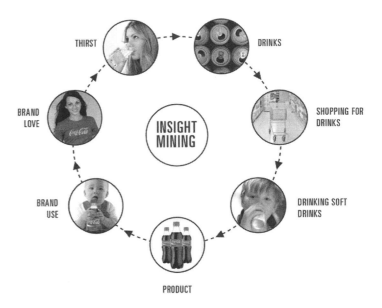

Shopping, the buying behavior, and how we can and do transact is a rich bed for insight discovery. Looking into things like convenience, times, volumes, portfolios shopped, influence of recency in messaging, spontaneity of purchases, how we navigate, which purchase behaviors exist and why, all unlock insight into how we buy. Even efforts of mining down to how we feel about value, price, rewards, and promotions can offer worthwhile insight.

Next, we look at how we might consume within the category. The underlying platforms here include how we interact with competitors and why we use certain products and sometimes in different ways. We also look deeply into how consumption of products in that category makes us feel. Do we get a special lift from the bubbles in soda? Do we hold our face close to the glass so the bubbles tickle our nose? Do we drink fast to belch? Is thirst satisfied quickly or slowly? Which feelings are produced from these interactions: joy, indulgence, satiation, naughtiness, or refreshment? And why is that the case? Do some brands give us feelings that are different from others and if so, why?

When it comes to your product, it is important to look at how it is used within its intended fashion. Here we could be looking for consumption insights like: Do we consume a lot of it—when and why? What factors influence the way we use the product? How do we feel? Why do we drink Coke? Do we feel different than when we drink comparable beverages? And again, why?

Unintentional brand use is yet another dimension to explore. You may find interesting insight when poking through the ways in which people use products differently than their intended use. Here we can connect the brand and consumers on a special level because the diverse use of products can be insightful. For instance, you can look at the use of Coke for cooking or for curing nausea.[3] Then ask some more questions: How do we feel knowing this? Does everyone know? Are we inspired by versatility? Does the packaging hold special significance? Is it used for something else? Why? Follow those questions up with some more whys.

What about the brand itself—outside of the product? How does it make us feel? Why do we feel that way? Are we fans or consumers? What does the brand say about me? Is there status in the brand? Why? What about awareness? Is there cultural influence? What trends or styles exist around the brand? What is the social conversation and why? How does the brand resonate? Why?

**Revert to Age Five.** Five-year-olds get it. Have you ever noticed how kids at the age of five always ask "why?" They are at a stage in life when they seek knowledge and understanding because they don't have preconceived views from experience or a lifetime of learning. This fresh inquisitive nature is not jaded by what they already know like it is with us self-proclaimed experts. This unfiltered, and never satiated, perspective is truly a gift when looking for insights. So even when you think you know what the insight is, ask yourself and ask your teams, "Why is that the case? Why do consumers feel that way?" Become a five year old for a few minutes and see how that helps in apprehending the inner nature of things.

These are just some examples of the dimensions and questions we can explore. Not all will yield powerful consumer insight for emotional connection or storytelling but some will. The fun of it is that you just never know where the most valuable insight is going to pop up. With time and experience applied, the exploration becomes more focused. That said, you've certainly noted an important trend to apply during insight exploration: asking the question "Why?" Remember how Chapter 6 highlighted the value of asking why? during the process of Brand Purpose exploration? This why unlocks the emotions behind consumer feelings and actions. It is the most powerful word in the determination of insights. In our busy lives where we are constantly making decisions, we often forget to stop and explore the reasons and the triggers—the *whys*.

Understanding the sort of things we look for when mining for insights is a great start. Now here's some assistance with where and how to look for them. This is when research proves critical. In our opinion, research is most valuable when used to inform great thinking, rather than when trying to justify or assess great thinking.

The nature of the brand, the consumer, the product, and the environment all have an influence on the exact sources of insight. Here is a fairly simplified illustration as an example to show you what that looks like:

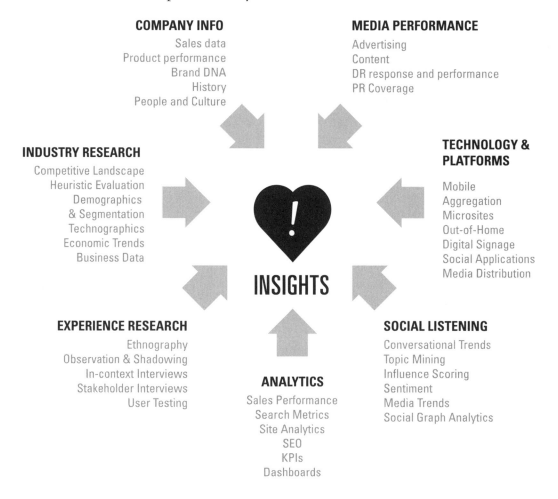

**COMPANY INFO**
Sales data
Product performance
Brand DNA
History
People and Culture

**MEDIA PERFORMANCE**
Advertising
Content
DR response and performance
PR Coverage

**INDUSTRY RESEARCH**
Competitive Landscape
Heuristic Evaluation
Demographics
& Segmentation
Technographics
Economic Trends
Business Data

**TECHNOLOGY & PLATFORMS**
Mobile
Aggregation
Microsites
Out-of-Home
Digital Signage
Social Applications
Media Distribution

**INSIGHTS**

**EXPERIENCE RESEARCH**
Ethnography
Observation & Shadowing
In-context Interviews
Stakeholder Interviews
User Testing

**ANALYTICS**
Sales Performance
Search Metrics
Site Analytics
SEO
KPIs
Dashboards

**SOCIAL LISTENING**
Conversational Trends
Topic Mining
Influence Scoring
Sentiment
Media Trends
Social Graph Analytics

Similarly, the methods you use are defined by the need. You can use qualitative methods to uncover what people say they do and use ethnographic fieldwork to uncover what they actually do. This includes the engagement of remote ethnography, mobile research, experience modeling, in-context interviews, and video and photo capture. Secondary research can lead to understanding cultural trends, demographics, industry changes, technology adoption, and media and trend analyses. Finally, quantitative research and analysis has taken leaps forward in both data and technology. We have resources that provide quantitative surveys and panels, which establish representativeness and significance of the brand and category. We can observe and adjust our business based on the behavior dynamics we learn about from technology-based tracking systems and modeling. We will discuss behavioral and experience research more in the next chapter because it's certainly an area of exploration for behavioral insight. Although quantitative data don't always yield insight into emotions, they can uncover areas that should be explored. For example, if a pattern of behavior is discovered when a product is used in a particular way and you ask "Why?", you can then unearth insight into brand influence, social status, or other emotional spaces.

Although research is a powerful tool, you should also maintain a healthy cynicism because not all the answers are not found in research. Don't take the numbers, statistics, and responses at face value. To find real insight, research these findings, explore, and discuss them even further. We also feel research is best used to inform thinking rather than to judge thinking. Testing messaging can be useful, but realize that testing anything after the direction is set will not create real and new insight, because it is based on an existing frame of reference. In other words, use your intuition and a healthy dose of cynicism with regard to research so you can ensure it's used in a meaningful way without overdramatizing what it says.

Think about what you're using it for and how you're doing it. Is a planned and moderated focus group the right way to gain insight into how people feel, or will that just give you what respondents want to say? Hugh Mackay, a renowned psychologist and social researcher, offers his view: "Focus groups are nothing more than a bunch of strangers, meeting in a strange place, saying strange things." Instead, what Hugh and his teams have very effectively done for years is conduct discussion groups in context of the normal lives of people, with friends, with neighbors or with work colleagues meeting in their natural habitats—the home of one of them, or a workplace, a club, or wherever they would naturally meet and feel most comfortable.[4] Here the research is more ethnographic in nature. It is observational and it studies the conversation arch, the participants, behaviors, and sentiment. It's a more immersive approach with less risk of strangeness diverting the discussion or findings. It's also highly nondirective.

The fact remains: Insight comes from understanding, and research is one great means to that end. Remember that because emotions are by no means rational (like a research method is), there are other means to connect with your consumers—through the use of intuition and insight.

We've talked our talk about consumer insights, so now let's explore how we've walked that talk.

> **INSIGHT:** "You don't truly experience something unless you immerse yourself in it."

This was an insight we uncovered about global travelers in partnership with the Tourism Queensland teams. This became part of the strategy behind our "The Best Job in the World" project created together with Tourism Queensland in

Australia.[5] This project achieved world acclaim for its ability to inspire billions of people across the globe to watch and follow the job applications for roughly 35,000 hopeful applicants, each of whom created hundreds of thousands of news articles and content pieces promoting Queensland's Islands of the Great Barrier Reef. The idea of "The Best Job in the World" was born out of the strong strategic insight that "you don't truly experience something unless you immerse yourself in it." Consumers all over the world seek greater value in the quality of experiences they have. "Fly and flop" types of vacations and holidays are diminishing. People want real experiences that they can share with friends upon return (and electronically while they are there). They want more than just seeing. They want to do, feel, and touch. They want to explore. They want to immerse themselves. As such, our insight territory tapped into the heart of the modern traveler—the traveler who sees potential on the Internet but knows they need to be immersed in that experience in person. What better way is there to be immersed in paradise than to live there—with a job, "The Best Job in the World?"

> **INSIGHT(S)**: "Competition in people, performance, and power" (The two-way player) and "Connection with culture and expression" (The avid player).

There were two consumer profiles for our work with the X Games. Each consumer audience engaged for different emotional reasons. We resolved to address both of them through experience and a single Organizing Idea. In this project, the two-way player was someone who loves the competition side of sports and watches it on TV. By contrast, the avid player loves action sports so much that he or she is part of the culture. Avid players live for the expressive nature and creativity of action sports, and they are out there perfecting "ollies" day in day out. In this project, we worked hard to build the Story System to connect with both players and to connect both players together through shared experiences and shared content. You can read more on the ESPN X Games story in Chapter 9.

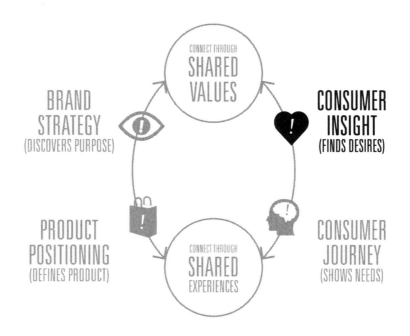

Now that we've explored the context of emotional connection and insights, where we look for them, and how to look at them, let's think about how insight serves as a pillar for the Organizing Idea. Using this new and vast understanding of your consumer, look for consumer insight into desire. This emotional desire can inspire a story for your Brand Purpose and become the conduit for connection with consumers. This insight provides a consumer frame of reference for the

Organizing Idea. Remember: We are looking for "a revelation about human behavior or an emotion that can be leveraged to connect a brand" or "a new usable perspective on the relationship between a brand and its existing or intended consumers." Insight enables you to understand people and situations in a very clear way. Make your work both inspiring and focused—and of course, be insightful.

# IN THEIR SHOES

*Using Ethnography to Understand Consumer Engagement and Buying Insights*

# IN THEIR SHOES

*Using Ethnography to Understand Consumer
Engagement and Buying Insights*

While most of the world was suffering some form of financial crisis, we were
helping a fast casual restaurant chain to reposition its brand and reengage its
consumer base. The financial crunch had a strong impact on people eating out,
which made the pleasure of taking the family out for dinner limited to special
occasions. The once affordable save-mom-from-cooking family outing became an
indulgence.  Outside of weekends when there was excess demand, the mid-week
casual dining customers were staying at home. More than ever, the competition for
restaurants was the supermarket (with huge marketing budgets), which promoted
great-value family-friendly meal options for consumers to cook at home. As a
result of these and many other factors, the way consumers considered and looked
at the fast casual dining category had changed. We needed to effectively relearn
how to market to a changed consumer dynamic. We needed to reenergize the Brand
Purpose, enhance and connect the consumer experiences, freshen the brand story,
and amplify the social conversation. All in service of increasing foot traffic and
check size.

**To Eat with You Is to Know You.**  Part of our challenge was to deeply
understand consumers in this new dynamic: how they make dining decisions, how
they feel about the experience, what their needs are, and most important, why. We
had to walk in their shoes to understand their lifestyles, their wants, and needs,

along with all their associated emotions both across and through the Experience Space. The best way to do this was to embark on a journey of great discovery. Therefore, in addition to traditional secondary research, our teams started dining at the restaurant. When our teams returned with photos, stories of their experiences, insights, and observations of consumers, SapientNitro reimbursed their costs. Some of our team members even went so far as to work shifts in the restaurant, and during each shift, they video-interviewed their restaurant mentor. After gathering all of this direct front line information, we mapped the consumer journey and detailed what we considered key stages of the consumer experience. Then, with an experienced ethnography researcher, we studied and explored consumer experiences. We interviewed families at home while they were having dinner to better understand that experience and how they felt about it in comparison with eating out. Next, we performed entry and exit interviews at restaurants to capture expectations and reflections. Last, our researcher dined in the restaurant with families and couples—making notes of observation, recording conversations and behaviors, and studying how consumers felt along the journey. We used all of this information to map dimensions of the experience, define opportunities, and unearth insights. These were the insights that were embedded at the intersection of behavior and emotion, or what consumers did and how they felt. All of which was immensely valuable input for Storyscaping a new world of experience.

**At the Peak of Anticipation.** One of our newly discovered insights ended up being paramount in our strategy for social amplification. It is natural to think that the best time to stimulate a positive social conversation about a restaurant experience is right after dining—upon completion of your meal, when you're leaving, on your way home, or upon arrival home. However, during this phase of our project, it was only after literally getting into the shoes and minds of our consumers that we discovered the exact opposite was true. In this case, the restaurant's fast casual dining style included extensive pasta, salad and dessert bars—each offered buffet style. This eating arrangement triggered the height of emotional connection during the anticipation stage while diners contemplated which combinations of options to feast on and how they could create any taste sensation or side they wanted. And, there's more! These consumers could have multiple desserts separately or in one bowl, reaching their creative peak with ice cream and chocolate sauce, bacon chips and jalapenos—all plausible options. At the tail end of the consumer journey, we found the exact opposite of what one might expect to be a fully positive experience. After dining, customers certainly were satisfied, yet also burdened with remorse. Remorse for eating more than normal, remorse for partaking in that wacky combination they felt they just *had* to try, remorse for consuming one too many desserts. Contrary to expectation, social amplification at the end of the journey was likely to be a negative, while conversation of anticipation would more than likely inspire positive consideration. Both of these were strong emotional states tied to behavior and the experience. Had we not walked in the shoes of these consumers using ethnography and research, these and many other insights would have been left to our imaginations and, perhaps, our assumptions. In this case, we drew on many insights throughout the consumer journey in a full-on effort to successfully understand consumer needs—living out the key reasons (the how and why) they used the restaurant's products and services to satisfy themselves. All this is pertinent information used in the Storyscaping approach. We also used one core insight as a pillar for determining the Organizing Idea: Our individual tastes are as diverse and different as we are.

This is just one quick story of how getting into the shoes of consumers opened up a world of insight we would never have seen from our position on the outside looking in. For us, ethnography and other associated research practices are fundamental in building environments, tools, products, and content—all things that enable the immersive experiences that consumers expect today.

**Start with People.** Now let's explore the principals and practice of ethnography and associated research to get a better grip on how we can more clearly understand consumers and their choices along their journey. Our premise is that people have experiences and that brands mobilize communications, products, services, environments, and more, to shape those experiences. Experience, in this sense, emerges from ongoing patterns of perceptions and interactions, and we cast aside the portrayal of consumers as detailed personas surrounded by touch points. Instead, we start with people on their own terms rather than as a series of homogenous demographics pushed through a sales funnel projecting a single possible outcome—consumption. Storyscaping is built on a significantly deeper understanding of consumers and their relationship with the brand through their experience. In fact, this understanding should go as far as being an "always-on" understanding—more on that later.

Although we recognize that, in reality, consumer emotion (as explored in our consumer insight pillar) and this pillar of understanding needs and behavior are inextricably linked, we separate them purely from a logical viewpoint so that you can see how a brand can be connected on an emotional level. That's what brand storytelling tries to do, which is different than when a brand tries to interact with something. Part of brand interaction is giving consumers a benefit that solves some sort of need. Since that need could be emotional, realize that you cannot separate emotional and functional need in perfect terms because they are connected. We look at these pillars specifically and individually in their two dimensions in an effort to enable deeper understanding and ensure Organizing Ideas and Story Systems, which are better informed.

**Behaviors Are Storytellers.** What do we mean by *understanding consumer engagement*? What are we saying when we talk about "buying insights?" Needs are something that can be solved; and when we link that to understanding consumer engagement, we are saying that it is not a matter of finding a square hole so you can build a square peg to put in it. When we talk about understanding those needs it's not just knowing what the need is, it's about knowing why that need exists and understanding that it is connected to many other elements and dimensions of a person's life. It's also about recognizing that sometimes that need isn't conscious—it could be biological. And, as we discussed in the section on product/service positioning, utility needs may even have strong unconscious habitual characteristics (in which case we would study the influences of the habit, the context, the perceived outcomes, etc. rather than just the habitual behavior and functional need). By studying needs and behaviors through meaningful research, we also identify the interconnection with the realms of self-identity, culture, brand value, and Brand Purpose—the realms of the symbolic. Here we are looking at needs and behaviors as the way in which these things become real and have manifested for the consumer. It is in our behavioral routines, in the ways we interact in the world, and in the products or services we plug in that tell our story about who we are or what we want to do. This holds true whether it is a deeply considered decision (such as what to feed your cat—c'mon, you know people can be obsessively particular about this), and when it's one of the plethora of decisions we make which are made barely above the level of perceptibility (such as your choice of socks this morning—you just reached in the drawer and grabbed a pair that was a consistent color with your pants).

Research helps reveal how we are using the products that companies make and sell and how we tell stories to one another about who we are. In that storytelling, we gain additional ideas and discover new ways to be who we are. We are always looking for ways to make those stories fresh and more compelling; therefore, we need to continually understand consumers, their frames of reference, their language, and their expressions.

**Need to Move Beyond Need.** All too often the concept of understanding consumers has been reduced to just identifying their needs and market research has become a kind of dreaded hurdle that must be cleared before you go on to the next phase of development. Or in the worst cases, a "validating needs" approach is applied which acts like a screen that is so finely meshed nothing but absolute mediocrity passes through it. Similarly, using arbitrary gatherings of isolated and uncontextualized data (like social listening sentiment) to understand consumers is nothing more than a charade. We believe it is more important to explore something one of our thought leaders in this field calls, "answers of uncertainty." Dr. Rick Robinson, vice president, marketing analytics—IOTA, describes this as, "The things you find out which result in someone saying 'maybe it's . . .' or 'it could be that. . .' or 'what might happen if. . . .'" In other words, it's an understanding of consumers that results in stories of possibility rather than in the reduction of risk, the elimination of uncertainty, or the validation of paths already taken.

Moving forward with this perspective on consumer needs and behaviors, we can now explore in more practical terms the principals and practices of ethnography to inform our understanding.

Ethnography is a core qualitative methodology within the field of anthropology and in simple terms, it is *the study of societies and cultures*. For our purposes, we are after a representation of the relationship between attitudes, perceptions, beliefs in the world, and the material world. In a commercial sense, the material world can be considered the interactions or behaviors with products and services, environments, and systems that are associated with our functional needs.

**Let's Go Hunting.**  The key to any research is defining where you start. In our commercial context, we need to think about it very practically. We cannot just grab a team of anthropologists and start out on a problem with a really wide range of discovery that will take two years to study. Instead, we have a practice that delivers the "Hunt," an approach that ensures you frame your work within a meaningful business context. Don't just do the discovery and then map on the business context later: Start with a hunt statement. The hunt statement is the overarching frame for the research—a broad or "global" statement of what we want to understand and why. It's a clear, concise, and compelling description of a project's most essential objectives. It provides a North Star for the research team, guiding the work by providing the team with clarity of Purpose. It reflects your understanding of the competitive landscape. Here is an example of a useful hunt statement:

> *Understand the families' experience of learning differences— particularly from the main caregivers perspective—in order to build an experience model that will inform both on and offline ABC Co. learning experiences.*

At its core, the hunt statement defines how the research addresses your business problem. By having the right hunt statement, the research is opened up for discovery while remaining contextually and commercially relevant to the business. It's also important to note that the business context should not be the brand's Purpose or product positioning because these are constraints. You really want to define a context for discovery that will identify opportunities to fill with the brand and products rather than the other way around.

Now that we've described the context for research, we can look at some models for planning. Our intention here is to give you practical understanding of how ethnographic research can aid consumer understanding, not to give you a PhD in research methods. We are just scratching the surface here in an effort to illustrate the value of using ethnography to understand consumer engagement and buying insights.

**Get a Bigger Slice.**  If you only look at what people are doing, you're only getting a narrow slice of the picture. If you only ask what people are thinking, you're only getting a narrow slice of the picture. Here you can plug in the expression "think, do, use" as a planning tool to anticipate how different elements of experience may interact in order to create routine observable behaviors. It is not meant to explain all experience. It is a visual tool—an aid to thinking critically. Each of the components—think, do, use—has an equal effect on the others. There is no hierarchy. It is not a cognitive model that says people think, and then they do, and then they use. It can be used to analyze both an individual's routine behavior and that of a collection of individuals—whether a user segment, a country, or a culture. From a working standpoint it is helpful to think about these two ways of using the tool, individually or collectively, as separate.

There are more heuristics and approaches to plan research and discovery. We could get into a long discussion around sampling the right people for research too, but we won't—we will just stick with a rather fundamental suggestion: The most important thing to remember with respect to sampling, no

## THINK

– How can we examine the cultural systems that underlie how people understand an experience?

– How do people frame their experience? How do people integrate new experiences into their old models of perception?

– Where are the points of possible intervention and changes in the ways in which people think about a brand, a product, a category, an experience?

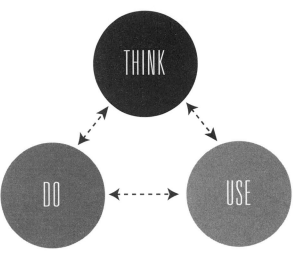

## DO

– What are people doing routinely?

– How is what they are doing informed by the frames they put around experiences?

– How is what they are doing informed by the material world they come in contact with?

– What are the points of intervention and possible opportunities in current routine behavior?

## USE

– What objects, tools, and products are people using to co-collaboratively create an experience with manufacturers?

– How do the attributes of these objects inform people of their intended use?

– In what unanticipated ways are users interacting with objects?

matter what method or approach is applied, is to ensure the sample is based on what you want to know and not on different user groups. Remember, we are trying to understand the relationship between attitudes, perceptions, beliefs in the world, and the material world—not solely the variables between one defined segment and another.

To bring this together, let's look at a case study where ethnography helped discover a cure for the common cold. Okay, it didn't cure the common cold, but it did inform the common cold experience model—a model that inspired and informed new product development and experiences for one of our clients. This client was lamenting the fact that the cold care category was oversaturated with products and there was nowhere for them to "move." The resultant opportunity map showed them that all of their products and their competitor's products fit in only one phase of illness. There was plenty of opportunity in the other phases— opportunities that were revealed by the cold care strategies their customers were engaged in during those phases.

We started by examining the common cold occurrence. Through the use of in-context qualitative research, we were able to identify a pattern in people's experience of having a cold. We then created a stunningly simple and intuitive four-stage model of the experience:

> **Something's Different** (SD) – *That tickle in the throat sort of feeling*
> **Getting a Cold** (GAC) – *My nose is starting to run*
> **Having a Cold** (HAC) – *It got me, I have a cold*
> **Getting over a Cold** (GOAC) – *Won't this ever end*

The current effort focused product almost exclusively on HAC. But clearly, there was more to say here. There were other ways of speaking to the same desired audience than, "Runny nose? Try this. Coughing? Try this."

HAC was where every cold care product was spending its marketing dollar. Instead, we explored having-a-cold as states of physical awareness. Awareness of a person's body, their mental state, and also their emotional states—each was heightened. Awareness of "being exhausted" or "mentally taxed" all went up and down. We mapped how people felt at different states to identify intersections of behavior and desire.

How people moved from one stage to another and what they felt within each stage is essential for rethinking how to frame messages for a cold care product. We did not examine user groups. We identified what we wanted to know—how do people experience a cold? Plotting the answers exposed us to fresh opportunities for approach, product enhancement, and increased market share.

We concluded that consumers were in the most positive and motivated state-of-mind during the Getting Over a Cold stage. Their desires for comfort and relaxation were heightened. We saw that they were in an active frame of mind to "do more to avoid getting sick again." They bore strong needs to strengthen and replenish themselves. This was all key to more effective strategy for the cold care product involved.

**Map Out the Opportunities.** One of the key applications of ethnography and establishing the experience model is the opportunity map. As illustrated in the cold care case study, the opportunity map is a powerful outcome of understanding the behaviors of your consumer and how products and services meet their needs. Opportunity maps can differ in how they are defined; most often they are illustrated as matrices. This matrix is an illustration of relationships that defines opportunities, based on your business objectives and the research findings.

Remember the restaurant chain we opened this chapter with? In that case, we explored opportunity by touch points along the journey and overlaid consumer emotional sentiment. The illustration here only shows one dimension of

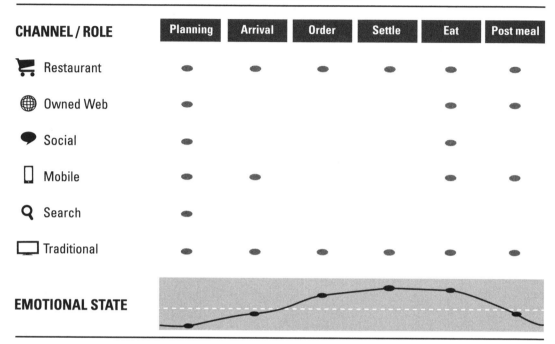

**THE BRAND'S POINT OF VIEW PROVIDES AN OVERALL FILTER & FOCUS**

the opportunities. Each dot was explored more deeply with consumer insights and product or service associations.

When we move beyond the traditional approaches to ethnography, we can leverage technology to gather data on behavior in new and meaningful ways. This does not make the more typical ethnography or research methods redundant, but it does have some commercial benefits in terms of data gathering and how we can understand consumers on new levels.

**You Know Something?** This is a new dimension of understanding the behaviors of consumer. To quote Geertz, "We use scientific imagination to bring us in touch with the lives of strangers."[1] Our aim is simply to understand deeply and find meaning in behavior through analysis of small slivers of everyday life. It's about people, places, and things. We deploy data gathering tools like sensors into the world for such research projects. These data gathering tools are anchored to people, places, and things. We draw quantitative and qualitative data. We tell stories and develop typologies of people and events, like the three types of mobile phone users or what a collaborative meeting sounds like. Our data consists of categories such as: noise levels, light levels, accelerometer data, temperature and humidity, Bluetooth, proximity, digital activity, surveys, and selective video. We use machine learning, statistics, and clever processing on large swaths of data to understand what we've collected. It's not necessary to know everything in efforts to know something.

In Japan, there is a thermopot (a fancy teapot) equipped with a special sensor.[2] It is used to help monitor the well-being of elderly who live at home alone. Why a teapot you ask? Many elderly people live alone and that has some risks. In many cases, someone visits and checks on them, which only gives you data based on that specific time when someone visits. With today's technology, we could have cameras watching and sensors on everything, or just on the teapot. The beauty here is that when the teapot is heated and lifted off the element, it sends a signal to a relative's smartphone to indicate that the elder is active. So imagine, the desire to know your mother is doing well can be solved by a sensor on her teapot. Why? Because you feel comforted when the teapot is making tea every day—that means she is up and at 'em and doing well. If she drinks tea at least three times a day, this sensor provides a practical and effective gauge, not to mention an elegant solution for the way instrumentation can give you the answer to the question you ask.

Like this example, the sensors we use are intentionally limited—low resolution, low sampling rate, restricted (but diversified) data types. Why? Privacy issues and avoiding analysis paralysis. Corroborating evidence helps us deduce meaning from activity, validates what we think we are seeing in the data, and adds richness through layers. And the gathering doesn't stop, which means we can better inform our goal for describing interaction, action, perception, and emotion, attention through interpreted stories and hard data.

Our project, Elder Care, is just such an example and one of various applications where we are using sensor based research to inform insights and opportunities. We started with the thought that we might be able to know something about when an elderly person's health shows a sudden decline. The hunt: *Develop a robust picture of daily living patterns within a specific elderly person's home, in order to identify changes in behavior or changes in bodily condition, which may suggest an emerging health problem.* Our approach: Kauth House is a study of an individual with chronic obstructive pulmonary disease (COPD) and more generally a pilot for the study of elderly in homes. We are establishing processes, protocols, and training materials for a broader community of study and also establishing benchmarks for understanding this individual with COPD. In order to identify changes in behavior or bodily condition, we must first establish a baseline to measure against. By establishing a "normal" set of behaviors and conditions, we will recognize abnormal conditions, which may signify a downturn in health.

A set of sensors were considered relative to the desired data sets, the environments, and the anticipated behaviors. A study of the activity zones was conducted and this informed sensor deployment.

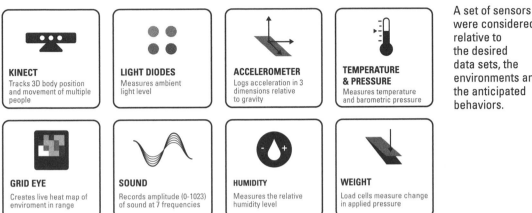

**KINECT**
Tracks 3D body position and movement of multiple people

**LIGHT DIODES**
Measures ambient light level

**ACCELEROMETER**
Logs acceleration in 3 dimensions relative to gravity

**TEMPERATURE & PRESSURE**
Measures temperature and barometric pressure

**GRID EYE**
Creates live heat map of enviroment in range

**SOUND**
Records amplitude (0-1023) of sound at 7 frequencies

**HUMIDITY**
Measures the relative humidity level

**WEIGHT**
Load cells measure change in applied pressure

A set of sensors were considered relative to the desired data sets, the environments and the anticipated behaviors.

Initial data visualization is being created to further refine the approach and establish base line norms.

Success in this research for insight means more than just hardware and research—it's a recognition that working within an always-on world of consumers requires a dynamic and constant exploration of the Experience Space. The mere fact that every smartphone has multiple sensors from GPS to accelerometers, light sensors, and the like, makes it possible to research our always-on-ness. Using the Internet as the platform, allows us to understand this world so we can better serve consumers and their stories.

**What You See Is What You . . .** Today, in order to fully realize the value of our research, the data, the findings, the interpretations, and the analysis should be illustrative. Ideally it should also be always on and dynamic. We believe the visual representation (dynamic and diagrammatic) of data is critical and key to effective interpretation. Today we can actually visualize almost all data layers. We have an aggressively creative stance toward using graphics and diagrams and even dynamic

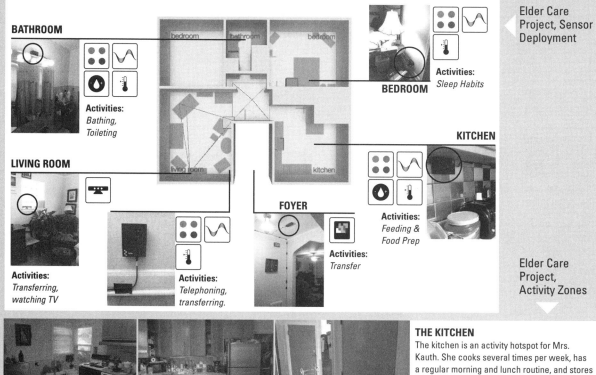

Elder Care Project, Sensor Deployment

**BATHROOM**

**Activities:**
*Bathing,
Toileting*

**LIVING ROOM**

**Activities:**
*Transferring,
watching TV*

**Activities:**
*Telephoning,
transferring.*

**FOYER**

**Activities:**
*Transfer*

**BEDROOM**

**Activities:**
*Sleep Habits*

**KITCHEN**

**Activities:**
*Feeding &
Food Prep*

Elder Care Project, Activity Zones

### THE KITCHEN
The kitchen is an activity hotspot for Mrs. Kauth. She cooks several times per week, has a regular morning and lunch routine, and stores her medicines mainly on the counter. **Activities to track include:** *feeding, typical morning habits, medicating*

### FOYER AND LIVING ROOM
Mrs. Kauth spends most of her time in the living room. She watches TV, eats her meals, reads, pays her bills, and talks on the phone from her favorite chair. The foyer, directly behind her chair, is the hub of the house. **Activities to track include:** *transferring, telephoning*

### THE BATHROOM AND BEDROOM
Mrs. Kauth has a very regular evening and morning routine. She wakes up around 9:30 am, showers several times per week, uses an oxygen machine every night, and heads to bed around 11 pm. **Activities to track include:** *bathing, dressing, toileting, transferring, sleep habits*

### KINECT VISUALIZATIONS

This moment shows Mrs. Kauth getting up out of her chair and walking towards the kitchen. It's 2:30 pm, so we may assume she's looking for a snack or afternoon medication. A lingering skeleton (in the back near a table) shows where a person previously had been. The red skeleton illustrates the most recent body position captured by the Kinect.

### GRIDEYE AND SPIDER (SOUND) VISUALIZATION

This moment shows sound in the voice-range from the Spider's microphone (column of circles) and a person walking through the foyer from the GridEye (heat map). Based on the path from the GridEye, Mrs. Kauth (who had previously been in her chair) entered the kitchen. The very dark spot in the heat map is caused by a radiator in the corner of the foyer.

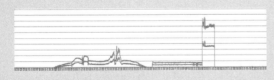

### SPIDER (LIGHT) VISUALIZATIONSPIDER (LIGHT) VISUALIZATION

This graph from Wed, 09 Jan 2013 06:08:40 to Thu, 10 Jan 2013 17:10:05 shows lights from sensor 2005 in Mrs. Kauth's bedroom. We can see when her lamp was on (peaks), ceiling light (low plateau), and ambient sunlight (long hill).

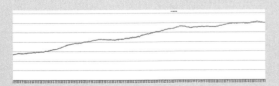

### SPIDER (BAROMETRIC PRESSURE) VISUALIZATION

This graph from Wed, 09 Jan 2013 06:08:40 to Thu, 10 Jan 2013 17:10:05 shows change in air pressure from sensor 2005 (bedroom). Low pressure means cloudy days. High pressure is usually a bit drier.

diagrams to represent each layer of data from raw data to interpreted models, like the experience model of the Sneezy case study. It is this visual representation that informs key insights or opportunities; and the defining of a key insight serves as the highlight of reference for the Organizing Idea.

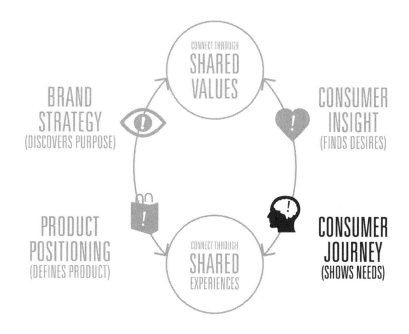

As with all four pillars, the strategies, insights, and findings of the pillar serve as valuable inputs for the Story System and development of Storyscapes, and we draw out one as a reference point for the Organizing Idea. For example, we studied the consumer journey in the health and beauty category, more specifically hair removal. It illustrated many emotional influences around self-esteem, social pressure, and what you would expect in the category. This pervasive range of options—all for one sliver of the segment—is mirrored by a constant desire to look and feel beautiful. As such, there is an ongoing expectation of the new and a desire for a simpler solution, while behavior showing commitment to a solution is often diluted by options and so-called innovations. Our core consumer insight was then defined as: "Confidence is my most powerful drug." This insight and understanding of the consumer's engagement behavior could now inform the Organizing Idea with greater relevance to how the brand can serve consumer needs in a competitive and cluttered context.

Now you have a solid grasp of Brand Purpose, product positioning, consumer insight, and consumer needs as they relate to Storyscaping. In the next chapter, we move on to offer a detailed definition of the Organizing Idea and how Systems Thinking is applied to create worlds of connected and immersive experiences. These are worlds that will be relevant and meaningful to consumers, their participation, and their evolution of their own personal stories.

# THE ORGANIZING IDEA

*Inspiring Experiences That Change Behavior
and Drive Transactions*

# THE ORGANIZING IDEA

*Inspiring Experiences That Change Behavior
and Drive Transactions*

We have now introduced the working model and all four pillars that hold up an Organizing Idea: Brand Purpose, product/service positioning, understanding of consumer emotions, and understanding of consumer needs. You've also learned the importance of and the difference behind creating a world instead of just creating ads. So now it's time to dig into one of the keys to unlocking the creation of your world—the Organizing Idea. Why? Because an Organizing Idea does just that; it organizes. Organizes what? you may ask. It organizes the connections between your consumer and your story in a way that builds emotional association and inspires behavior. It's a strategic input and sometimes, just sometimes, it may also be a creative expression. Organizing Ideas have the ability to help define how your brand interacts with the consumer. Even the very premise of what content you create, curate, or associate can be enhanced by leveraging it against an Organizing Idea. It's a powerful concept that unlocks great effectiveness in how your story is told, delivered, engaged with, and experienced.

Your Organizing Idea is built from the four pillars of insight and knowledge you develop around your brand and the consumer. We have covered each of these pillars in depth in the previous four chapters. Having a true and meaningful connection to your Brand Purpose is integral; your Organizing Idea becomes part of how you bring that Purpose to life. Without a connection to the Brand Purpose, your Organizing Idea is nothing more than another random idea.

As expressed in Chapter 6, the positioning of your product or service is an equally important pillar. You'll need a very clear perspective on what you offer, why you're offering it, and how you are going to deliver it; otherwise, the behaviors that you're seeking to create from Storyscaping will be less effective. The Organizing Idea serves to guide the type of experiences that are created and how those experiences are connected through a Story System. If you do not have a fundamental connection to the product or service positioning, everything you do will be less efficient in driving the ultimate response of a transaction.

The previous chapters on consumer insight prove how important it is to understand the emotional desires of consumers. The Organizing Idea fuels that emotional territory. To ensure the manner in which behaviors are inspired and immersive experiences are created, your Organizing Idea must have relevance and an association to consumer insight. This is key in keeping the desired connection in line with the purpose. Real consumer insight is often the foundation for the most creative solutions, particularly in the area of communication and the telling of the story. Truly understanding the emotional toils or cultural influences of a consumer is priceless. No amount of effort, exploration, or discovery is too much when it comes to finding fresh and authentic insight. It pays to explore all the dimensions of a consumer. We should explore at the widest level while taking the following into consideration: cultural insight, category insight, competitive insight, and the deepest level, insight into consumer emotion.

Finally, you gained a clearly defined view of how a consumer interacts with people, places, and things. Often illustrated as a consumer journey, knowing and following these interactions is foundational to understanding what and where behaviors exist. This information provides insight into how interactions may be harnessed, changed, or amplified. This effort is not as simple as looking at a day in the life of a consumer. We need to go deeper and understand the emotional journey and how that sentiment relates to their behavior.

Using these pillars, we can explore how to establish an effective Organizing Idea. First, we must understand what it is we are creating. We define an *Organizing Idea* as "an active statement that defines what the brand must do to change consumer behavior. It inspires the type of experiences that are created through the Storyscape."

An Organizing Idea is *not* a big idea. A big idea is the creative expression or the OMG experience that delivers on an Organizing Idea.[1] Red Bull is an amazing brand, a content brand that is connected with big ideas—really big ideas, like a guy riding a balloon to space and jumping out of it. Now that is a big idea, but it's not an Organizing Idea. Let's explore that a little. Red Bull has many big ideas, partnerships, content, and distribution channels.[2] How does it get value from them all? The value appears and appreciates because they are all connected to an Organizing Idea. An Organizing Idea for Red Bull could be something like "take flight," which is beautifully expressed as, "Red Bull Gives You Wings." Starting from an idea like "Red Bull Gives You Wings" gives you real options to organize around. That's why, when a crazy (in a good way) guy wants to jump from a balloon in space, you say, "Hell yeah that works." It works because it is in line with your brand, it connects with your product through energy, it engages consumers that are content driven, and it excites emotionally. And even more than that, it brings to life the Organizing Idea of "Red Bull Gives You Wings." When you look at Red Bull Flugtag, Joyride, Cliff Diving, and X Games sponsorships, you see that many of its connections and associations link to its Organizing Idea. And most important, the role of product is undeniable. This enables each Red Bull experience to lead to another without brand disconnect, even though the experience may be around different content.

**Let the Creation Begin.** Creating an Organizing Idea is not a science; there is no formula. There are inputs and insights but not a formula that guarantees a great idea. If there was a formula, ideas would no longer be the outcome of creativity. What we can offer you is a way to test whether you have an Organizing Idea or not. We see it more as a craft—a craft that comes from the input of many people. It's a recipe of sorts—the main ingredients being instinct, gut feeling, experience, and passion—mixed into a melting pot of opportunity. The way you want to approach this dish is by finding a balance between being strategically minded, and at the same time, inspiring. That's why it's a craft; it's built on teamwork.

We utilize an approach called connected thinking, where the outcomes of multiple opinions from different dimensions are more powerful than the view of

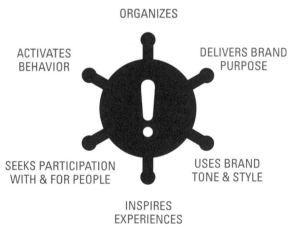

ORGANIZES

ACTIVATES
BEHAVIOR

DELIVERS BRAND
PURPOSE

SEEKS PARTICIPATION
WITH & FOR PEOPLE

USES BRAND
TONE & STYLE

INSPIRES
EXPERIENCES

one lone genius. That's not to say that having a genius contribute isn't valuable, of course it is, but it's just one dimension. An Organizing Idea has multiple perspectives supporting it. At the same time, an Organizing Idea has a far-reaching application. This is why connected thinking is a critical foundation for ensuring the exploration of opportunities, while ownership of the idea remains shared. Plus, this process of collaboration builds understanding among people from the outset.

When crafting and creating an Organizing Idea, we are looking for key characteristics that deliver on the pillars.

**Here are some initial questions to ask yourself as you try to develop your Organizing Idea:**

– Does it organize? Does it clearly give you a premise to organize how consumers will connect with the story?

– Does it help define the role of the channels you will use?

– When you hear it, do you feel like it activates behavior? You're looking to stimulate an experience for consumers and these experiences require a behavior.

– Is the Organizing Idea, along with the associated projected experiences, delivering on the Brand Purpose? That is, does it align with and activate your brand's belief? You should be able to draw a very clear logical connection between what the Brand Purpose is and what the Organizing Idea is all about. A good perspective comes from also asking yourself, Is the expected emotional connection in line with the brand cause, belief or Purpose?

– Brands are more than messages; a brand is a personification of a company. This personification should make you more likeable, memorable, and desirable for consumers. Similarly, an Organizing Idea should be in sync with and even a proponent of the brand's tone and style. You can easily and quickly ask yourself, Does it sound like the brand would say this?

– Remember, the goal is to inspire immersive experiences. When you think about your Organizing Idea, do you instantly feel like you can create an experience that will deliver the behavior?

– Finally, Storyscaping is about building a world of immersive experiences and participation. An Organizing Idea is a core platform of experience, and as such, it needs to seek participation, either overtly or through likely behaviors. It's a hard ask, but it's one worth considering: Does the Organizing Idea have the potential to inspire experiences where people will involve the brand in their stories?

We've offered a series of aspects that we look for in an Organizing Idea, but again, it isn't a science. Assessing a few words of thinking is not a definitive task. This is why experience, multiple perspectives, and forethought are applied. You have to imagine the creative expressions and experiences that the Organizing Idea is part of. Often the Organizing Idea is not formed in isolation of exploring creative expressions and territories. It's not a passing-of-the-baton process between an Organizing Idea to a big idea and so on. It's an organic, interactive, and creative process.

**What to Avoid.** Creating an Organizing Idea is a new concept. We have explained how it differs from a big idea. From a strategic point of view, sometimes it helps to explore what to avoid. So, here are some things to watch out for when creating your Organizing Idea.

– Do not use a proposition. That is, a statement about a brand feature or benefit and will not serve to organize. Instead, it should be an expression that inspires and changes behavior—not an offer that aims to manipulate. In other words, don't use phrases like, "Only Sue Generic pizza has a family made special sauce," or "Buy one pizza, get one free, only at Sue Generic pizza."

– Do not use a bland or obvious statement. Our aim is to inspire creativity that connects with sharp insight. In other words, don't use expressions such as, "Increase the preparedness of our fans and customers," or "Help our customers do more."

– Do not have it come from a consumer insight or consumer point of view. We seek to connect with consumers through insight, because insights inform Organizing Ideas. It shouldn't sound like a description of a consumer's world or desires. In other words, don't use insights such as, "I seek balance in all dimensions of my life," or "You can only fully immerse yourself in a place when you live there."

– The principal purpose for and the creation of an Organizing Idea requires a fundamental shift in perspective. It's at the very center of Storyscaping because it enables the development of connections for Story Systems and helps define channel roles, points of engagement, story dimensions, priorities, and experience opportunities.

If you are now starting to think about what your brand's Organizing Idea might be or have done so while reading this chapter, you are right on track. If not, then please begin that process. If you have identified an Organizing Idea but are not sure whether it is right, just keep in mind that capitalizing on the power of an Organizing Idea requires some organizational shift in perspective. If you are not able or willing to define decisions around how to deliver your brand, build experiences, create content, tell stories, plan media, or define commerce channels with an Organizing Idea, you risk the true effectiveness that can be achieved. This is where we see many organizations are being challenged. Use this challenge as your fuel for positive change within your company. Believe in an Organizing Idea and strong Purpose that drives and builds immersive experiences—doing so can catapult organizations to new levels of efficiency and effectiveness and even increase the value of brands and your business as a whole.

Over the last decade, Coca-Cola unearthed the power that a strong application of Purpose and an Organizing Idea can achieve. And they still never sacrifice creativity, story evolution, or consumer engagement. Back in 2003, the Coca-Cola brand used the slogan, "Coca-Cola . . . Real" but there were many different ad campaigns that played out around the world. In 2005 they adopted the slogan, "Make it Real" and continued with a variety of diverse advertising campaigns across the world, and the casual observer could think that the brand and slogan were the only link between them. But in 2006 they started to consolidate as a global brand around the positioning of "The Coke Side of Life"[3]—a powerful, consumer-relevant idea. A couple of years later, you could start to see how the brand was more consolidated to the idea, not just the tagline. A few more years down the road the work became more aligned to their Purpose, when they focused around the Organizing Idea of "Open Happiness." Now the majority of marketing effort appears to be behind one idea platform.[4] They continue to create many different and great stories and experiences of the brand, and you can see they are all true to "Open Happiness." This illustrates that Coca-Cola has streamlined globally—from having many different communication ideas and ad campaigns only connected by the slogan—to being centered around one core idea. Can you imagine the impact and effectiveness that would come from this global level consolidation, as consumers are more globally connected? Oh, and if that wasn't enough value, please also note, their share price is 174% of what it was in 2003.[5]

Now that you have an understanding of the strength and importance of an Organizing Idea, let's explore how to apply an Organizing Idea within the creation of Story Systems.

## ESPN X Games: *An Awe-Inspired Organizing Idea*
**CASE STUDY**

With X Games (part of the ESPN world) expanding rapidly to host six events per year (from three) and taking their events global in 2013, we were faced with a few specific business challenges:

First, we had to invent new ways to distribute more content to more markets as part of a new digital suite. Second, we were charged with maintaining the premium status of the X Games brand within the world of action sports. Fundamentally, we had to create a world of experience to engage fans through user-generated content (UGC) and branded content keeping the X Games on the forefront of technology as well as sports. And with the global expansion, X Games called on us to help them grow their audience. Of course, this global audience created other strategic hurdles like content coming in from mixed markets; so part of our planning process involved mapping the markets to demonstrate how they could be linked. Finally, and perhaps most important from the client's point of view, we were challenged to increase revenue by raising both site visits and user engagement.

**Action and Inspiration.** The Organizing Idea behind creating a new world for X Games was simply "Activate Awesome." What this inspired was by no means simple. The foundation of the Organizing Idea was a collaboration of many people and truly displays connected thinking at play.

We were provided with a clear Brand Purpose for X Games: "bring new and go huge." The campaign to communicate would be built on this offer. We aimed to connect and to inspire even more action and even more immersion in the experiences.

The product offer was also clear, with X Games expanding in markets and in content with the addition of new events and activities ranging from film competitions to the Big Air.

We then set out to understand our consumer. Our insight approach focused in large part on our two main target groups: "avid" fans who were already action sports loyalists and "two-way players"—general sports fans who would tune in for large scale action sports events (mostly via TV). Research into these targets yielded key information regarding how technology plays a role in their lives, how they consume and use sports content (and why), where the broadcast and entertainment trends intersect with their behaviors, and what the existing conversation landscape was for X Games and competitive sports on the whole.

Through this process we found out that our avid fans connected more on the basis of a subculture of expression, with creativity and personal accomplishment serving as core motivations. Our two-way players connected more on the basis of competitive sport, with a bigger focus on newsworthy performance and the broader spirit of competition.

Next, we mapped out the engagement landscape. This started with a global look at the technology our fans used—everything from Internet-enabled TVs to smartphones and tablets—and just as important, how they used technology in tandem with the standard broadcast. This second-screen approach was a big part of a successful launch for us by recognizing the value that a second point of contact could bring by immersing people in the experience rather than creating broadcast redundancy. Our engagement insights helped us establish a vision for transforming passive viewing into active experiences.

It became clear that we had to "Activate Awesome" on many levels. So, we set out to make X Games the home of more than just an action sport. We became the home of ACTION. This involved making all events more connected to the fans by engaging them across a digital platform where X Games would be available to them no matter where they were—the couch at home, the mountaintop of Tignes, or a skate park on the street.

X Games are big and bold by nature, with athletes striving to bring innovative new tricks and their own sense of style. It is this combination—modern engineering paired with artistic expression—that inspired our visual design for the new X Games digital world. We took an app-first approach to design and focused on tablet and mobile experiences to define our interface and navigation styles. In short, making sure that X Games could evolve to become cutting edge without losing its edge.

**Activating the Experience.** We started with the X Games second-screen tablet app, which extended the viewing experience for the fans who were at the event and for the fans who were viewing and participating anywhere else. We connected the two audience groups in an unprecedented way!

The connective feature that we introduced is called The HypeMeter—a real-time interactive engine (live during X Games events) that measures at-event, at-home, social, and gaming buzz to boil each moment of X Games down to a single score from 1 to 100. For the first time ever, fans at the event and fans at home could actually cheer together, adding hype through Twitter velocity, Facebook shares, and lightweight gaming through both the site and app experiences.

Through the use of a corresponding "hype chart," fans were then able to explore the biggest moments of X Games at a glance and access pieces of content that correlate to the biggest peaks. This means ESPN now has a new way to add a social layer of analysis.

Another key feature of the digital experience is Trick Track, a second screen experience that adds to the live broadcast by providing real-time trick names, statistics, and results—which means fans everywhere can engage with an entirely new level of information. So, from your couch at home, you can now feel like you are in a fan seat and in a judge's seat, bringing you closer to and deeper inside the action.

It's one thing to design a new world; it's another to build it into an interactive experience that brings together fans at home and fans at a live event—across social content, broadcast, and action—in one space. We believe that is the power of an Organizing Idea. This one inspired us to change the way that fans actually engage with the sports and the athletes they love.

**Immersed Like Never Before.** By "Activating Awesome" in a new world of immersive experience, we generated a depth of engagement never before realized. At launch, the app was number one for 12 days in the iTunes store. Over the full year, all digital engagement measures from uniques to time on site, and video plays, everything is up 100 percent or more.

Our partners at X Games were delighted with the results: *"The numbers were MASSIVE compared with those of last year. It was a great win for the brand, and we are extremely happy."*

Utilizing an Organizing Idea is a powerful new concept for marketing. With it, you can create worlds of experience that are inherently connected to the four pillars: your Brand Purpose, product and its positioning, the consumer on an emotive level, and the consumer on a behavioral level, from newly defined opportunities and insights. The next step is the application of an Organizing Idea to the Experience Space. It's where the Organizing Idea helps define the role of channels, the story line connections, and the types of experiences that matter.

# MEET YOUR STORYSCAPE

*When Your Organizing Idea and the Experience Space
Soulfully Meet*

# MEET YOUR STORYSCAPE
*When Your Organizing Idea and the Experience Space Soulfully Meet*

We all know that some things just go smashingly well together and sometimes their combination is better than the individual elements. It's the 1 + 1 = 3 equation. Take, for example, peanut butter and jelly, Vegemite and cheese, gin and tonic—all better when combined together. The combos hold more weight than connections; there is a soulful amplification effect. This is how we see the joining of Organizing Ideas and Experience Spaces. By bringing them together, we get a more meaningfully constructed and effective Storyscape—one that enables connections to more than a brand logo or design style. We achieve the creation of worlds that are connected through relevant stories, technologies, and experiences that the consumer becomes immersed in.

You have studied the overall model and approach for Storyscaping. Throughout your journey, you have uncovered your brand's Purpose uncovered a key emotional insight, uncovered a behavioral insight, and developed product or service differentiation that delivers big on these values. By connecting these four pillars, you have inspired an Organizing Idea. This is a powerful thing. Now we will learn how to soulfully connect the Organizing Idea and Experience Space to create a Story System and ultimately derive a Storyscape. To do so, we focus on the new applications in the model, the Organizing Idea and the Experience Space. We then apply Systems Thinking to build a Story System and ultimately derive the Storyscape.

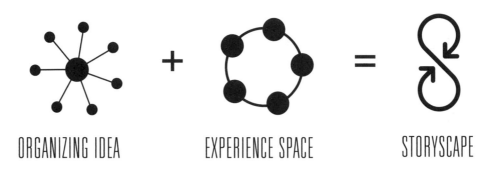

ORGANIZING IDEA     +     EXPERIENCE SPACE     =     STORYSCAPE

Let's start by digging into the Experience Space. Think of it as the canvas upon which you will work to create a Storyscape. The Experience Space is a three-dimensional canvas that we first need to define. This canvas holds more than just physical environments—it also includes the virtual ones people create. Here we see beyond just the experiences with the products and enjoy the immersion with content. This canvas showcases more than consumer connection with channels, it is also a place to show the technologies and platforms that connect the many points of the consumer experience. And this canvas, with all these components, is not just a media space; it also includes media channels. We have to change our perspective on all of these things, especially the well-worn world of media.

**The Trouble with Media Myopia.** We started this book by reinforcing that *story* is one of the most timeless and powerful weapons in our arsenal to connect brands and consumers. Another incredibly important weapon we all use is *media.* Unlike *storytelling,* which we consider to be a timeless craft, everything we know about *media* is fleeting or has an expiration date. The media landscape, which is a part of the world around us, is constantly changing and evolving, and so is the way we live. On the other hand, the human condition does not change much over time. People will always be people, but the world we live in changes every day. This is the reason our storytelling journey will continue on its path of evolution. We build on top of valuable lessons we have learned about *story* over time. Conversely, our media journey is not an evolution at all; rather it's about revolution. Practices from the past, so-called "best practices," preconceived notions, and muscle memory just get in the way.

Our perspective on media really started to change for us some years ago. In early 2004, we had a bit of a revelation about the media planning process that changed our perspective forever. At that time, we were buying a ton of media for *Citibank*. In fact, our agency was one of the top digital media buyers in North America. This gave us enormous leverage and we gained valuable experience. Most important, it provided a multitude of opportunities to learn in what was a relatively new space. We were working with a number of *Citi* business groups and they extended an opportunity in the student loans business. This client was a very progressive thinker and was looking for an agency partner that was "digitally centered." Their target was young college students, whom they assumed were always online. As part of our discovery, we sent a team of charismatic folks out with a video camera to capture some "person-on-the-street" interviews—a little ethnography, a simple conversation with desired consumers. Our intention was to gather a quick, real-world understanding about how students financed their education and their thought process. Because most of us, agency and client alike, had been out of school for a few years—or a lot of years—the reality was that we all had dated perspectives on the subject.

When we played back the video from the field, we observed and learned a hell of a lot more than we were expecting, and it proved our perspectives certainly were dated. We were vastly wrong about one key assumption—that college students spent a ton of time online. All our media tools told us they did, our preconceptions told us they did, and all available third-party research confirmed the same. What we found directly from students is that they don't spend much time online at all. They have superactive lives: studying, partying, dating, exploring the outdoors, and did we mention lots of partying? They don't have time to sit in front of a computer (remember in 2004, the Internet was available only on your desktop computer). With this discovery, further research showed that high school students spent lots of time online—most every demographic group did. Even little old ladies spent more time messing around on their computers than college students. When it came to computer usage, our video interviews also revealed one hugely consistent thing—our students used their computers for *MySpace*. None of us had even heard of MySpace, and we were the ones who were expected to be hip to these trendy social happenings. In fact, 90 percent of our interviewees from different campuses mentioned MySpace. This revelation was not a "hidden gem" of an insight. It was the obvious, brought to light for anyone who simply took the time to ask. It changed the way we looked at media forever. What we learned, and this is foundational to the concept of Systems Thinking, was quite simply to understand the Experience Space of now, not just the media data of yesterday's perceived behavior. The world around us is changing constantly and media data tools are just a subset of our personal world; the media consumption data is a subset of that. In short, defining your canvas based on a database with an incomplete and dated perspective gives you a small flat space—not a three-dimensional dynamic world. And, the bonus of this discovery? We had the thrill of buying some of the first ads on MySpace (basically the first ads in social media), and they were rather effective too.

**Bring Back the Art.** Back in the *Mad Men* era we could count the TV, local radio stations, and print publications on our fingers and toes. The folks in the media department were cultural junkies who read every TV script. We were attuned to the editorial calendars at every publication. We were all consumers of all the same content. These folks were "agents." Along came the explosion of media outlets and the foothold of fragmentation where hundreds of cable channels and millions of websites popped up overnight—these certainly changed the media placement scene. It's virtually impossible to keep up with that level of marketplace understanding. Today you would describe a 20-something planner as one who sits in front of a screen, punching in some demographic parameters: *males, 24–30 that make $50,000+*, perhaps some psychographic parameters: *likes fishing;* and roll in segmentation filters: *has purchased a car in the last 12 months.* Click Enter and wait (a nanosecond) for a list of media venues, which index high across this "target audience." This person then sends those "just right" outlets a request for proposal, receives some pricing, and creates a spreadsheet for the media buy. Then, that spreadsheet gets tweaked. Finally, a little legwork and some negotiation is completed before the spreadsheet is turned into a PowerPoint deck and presented to the client for approval. We oversimplified this for the sake of making a point, but where the hell is the art in this? Where are the insights and the science? It's obviously flawed. An assumption, built on an assumption, built on another assumption is not science. Are all the possible media outlets and all the possible experiences or interactions in that database? MySpace certainly was not.

We reinforce the point here that media planning databases are a crutch that we should not solely depend on, and the media landscape changes so fast that any book you write on the subject today will be considered a history book tomorrow. Furthermore, media channels only exist in one part of the consumer's world; they do not encompass it all. We need to get out of the office and go walk in the shoes of our consumers in order to inventory and understand their world (their Experience Space). Only then can we define the canvas upon which you will create your Storyscape. Let us reiterate: A media plan is *not* that canvas; it's only a small part of it.

**Inventory the Experience Space.** Although we like the "paid, owned, earned" approach to media better than the status quo, even this is still not perfect. We believe it aligns more closely with how you should think about the Experience Space, but it too falls short. To us, an obvious gap opens when considering a view of the world as built around the brand's ecosystem versus building the Experience Space model around the consumer's ecosystem. Consider for a moment how making that seemingly small shift in context would have uncovered the role that MySpace played in those college students' lives in 2004. This same gap exists in connections planning as it is routinely done with a "brand out to consumer" lens instead of a "consumer out to world" perspective. Our goal is to understand the consumers' world and, with that knowledge, craft ways in which a product or service can be invited into it.

In Chapter 8, we offered a glimpse into the kind of primary research tools and methods we use to inventory the entire list of key touch points between your brand and its potential customer. By combining those findings with media planning data, you will end up with a bit more than an all-inclusive list. You will possess a valuable consumer journey map in the form of a matrix. This is a huge leap forward from connections planning. You now have a current view of the consumers' world, which extends way beyond paid media. The challenge now is focus and prioritization. We all have limited time, budget, and staff—how could we possibly do so much? Isn't it easier to just crank out another TV commercial? Or not? And that's why we believe this is a great practical benefit of the Storyscaping approach.

In fact, the reactions we get to this particular dimension of Storyscaping are off the charts. Although we don't believe you can build a great brand with a spreadsheet, we emphasize that this is the part where utilizing one becomes very handy. Businesses are clearly struggling with the number of tactics, channels and needs for new capabilities this digital world is throwing at them. Budgets are not growing as fast as the number of things businesses feel they need to keep up with: "We need a Facebook presence. Not just one, one for each product, and what are we doing with Twitter, Instagram, Vine, Tumblr? We need to be more mobile. Where's that app? What about upsell? And let's not forget YouTube! Let's do that, and have our own channel . . ." Dramatized? A little. A real challenge? Definitely. This model really helps you manage this challenge.

**To See or To Leave Be?** Which touch points should we focus on? What can we do with Pinterest? Should we invest in redesigning our website, or should we focus on our Facebook presence? Is our mobile platform effective? These are much more relevant questions to ask and they serve a greater Purpose than just building more stuff and disseminating more content. All of these questions are much easier to answer if you have a current understanding of the consumers' environment and experience. You are probably wondering how you can solve for nonlinear experience paths and reduce the number of touch points for which you create content or build either digital or physical experiences. Or, you may be trying to grasp the role of the channel in the consumer's world.

Our goal here is to define a model of the Experience Space that enables dynamic adaption, adjustment, and evolution. More on that later, but for now we need to understand and dig into the stages of creating a Story System. These are:

1. **Cast:** List all existing and potential touch points or channels.
2. **Score:** Add prioritization criteria through data sets.
3. **Tag:** Define the role of channels relative to scores scores, types, and roles.
4. **Inspire:** Connect your Organizing Idea and inspire stories, tactics, systems, platforms and solutions.
5. **Optimize:** Connect the points with technology and messaging.

It's a pretty straightforward process, but the value is in how you manage each stage.

1. **Cast:** Our goal is to list all of the probable touch points. As discussed earlier in this chapter, you will draw on your primary research and media planning tools to maximize this list and ensure it is relevant to the consumers of today. Leverage the opportunity mapping, the experience modeling, and the customer journey you have used to understand the potential points of connection and interaction. Use media tools in association with real-world data to build a complete list of probable and opportunistic touch points. List them out (probably in a spreadsheet).

2. **Score:** This is where strategic analysis kicks in. (Note, the criteria in the sample table that follows—*cost per reach, engagement, influence* and so on—are just for illustrative purposes and are a few of the common data points that you could use for scoring.) Establish a series of relevant data points and scoring weights based on what you are trying to accomplish. Obviously, they need to include the dimensions of effectiveness for your brand or product, which will be drawn from the understanding of the consumer and insights. Of course, you will always need some dimension of engagement, as that is a foundational element of a Storyscape in which we are building a world of immersion that needs engagement. You might also consider using levels of participation to score relative consumer involvement if that is the best way to achieve your business goals. Another dimension may include the emotional influence on your consumers along their journey. Your optimal levers and criteria should be logically tweaked to determine what touch points will dominate your Storyscape.

Add these dimensions and scores to the spreadsheet. Essentially, you will be creating a scorecard by touch point and channel in order to determine relative priorities.

The ultimate goal is to determine the priority of channels and touch points based on effectiveness in achieving your goals or objectives. For example, if you happen to have an older, well-known but perhaps tarnished brand and a great new product or service that needs to be experienced, in order to change those perceptions, you could set your model to optimize for cost-per-reach with maximum engagement. Let's explore that as a "completely redesigned and shiny new car." Start with scoring 1 to 10 for engagement. The highest level of engagement happens when a person is actually sitting in the car, gripping the steering wheel with both hands, smelling the leather, and hearing the engine roar while they take that last corner on their test drive—that experience earns a score of 10. Coming across a banner ad while checking your e-mail at work earns a 1. In relative terms that might score a TV spot as a 5, and an awesome TV spot could earn a 6.

**BUILDING YOUR EXPERIENCE SPACE:** sample spreadsheet

| PROBABLE TOUCH POINTS | *Prioritization Criteria** | | | | STORY SYSTEM |
| --- | --- | --- | --- | --- | --- |
| | *Reach* | *Cost/Reach* | *Engagement* | *Influence* | |
| Website | 4 | 6 | 8 | 9 | Town Center |
| Radio | 8 | 3 | 3 | 3 | Signpost |
| Search | 7 | 5 | 1 | 2 | Signpost |
| Pinterest | 1 | 9 | 5 | 4 | Roundabout |
| Facebook | 3 | 7 | 4 | 5 | Destination |

**\* Sample Criteria** — this should be customized according to the brand and business objectives.

Alternatively, if you were launching a new brand, you may look at a very different set of optimizing criteria. Pure reach might be more valuable, likewise with frequency. Are you clear on what you are trying to accomplish? If so, the formula you choose to utilize in efforts to identify the optimal experience will be relatively easy and straightforward to develop. It is important to always look for multiple criteria that match up both your business objectives and the principals of Storyscaping—such as engagement, immersion, and participation. Otherwise, you will end up with a one-dimensional brand first system, or worse, a broadcast only system that has no room for consumer involvement.

A powerful application of this approach is that you can be dynamic and adjust the scores based on performance data. The world of media and its role in how we connect and engage constantly changes, so this should be a working dynamic approach—not a plan and set-aside map. Make it dynamic, and evolve your Story System structure and priorities to be in line with what works and what doesn't or as you change the content, the systems, and platforms.

3. **Tag:** Through score-carding, as just explained, the point that not all channels or touch points are the same is reinforced. Beyond effect, cost, and whatever other dimension you score, they vary by nature and by the role they play in the Experience Space. At the broadest level, we can define channels by the roles they play relative to each other and by depth and type of engagement. We created a simple framework for this so we can tag touch points and channels with their optimal role.

This step is an important one and you must do it in order to assemble a Story System. Feel free to change the language to suit your style.

We imagine a roadway system to explain Story Systems: Each one has signposts, roundabouts, destinations, and town centers. Remember, the idea here is to ensure there are no dead ends for a consumer's journey. All roads lead to "town centers, and destinations" where you can engage with other people and content and buy the things you need or want. Call these four elements whatever you would like—as long as you understand the role and the reason each of these elements is meant to play.

**Signposts.** These are the easiest to understand because, for the most part, they resemble traditional ads—except these never end with a period. They always lead somewhere else, which is why they need to end with a comma. They have a clear and important job to accomplish: They must intrigue and entice a person to engage with the brand and encourage an experience. Total reach, cost-per-reach, frequency, and influence will play a big role in determining which of these will make it onto your plan. These ads serve to build awareness and drive acquisition and ultimately direct people to even greater engagement—like a signpost. These can include TV, radio, print, advertorial content, out of home, merchandising, banners, search terms, and so on. You get the point.

**Roundabouts.** These are the places where a customer or prospect may cross through during their journey. This could also be where they seek out information or inspiration related to your brand's world. Keep in mind that, it's likely you don't have the time or budget to create a significant experience at every spot where your brand and the consumer could potentially connect. Therefore, some of the touch points you uncover can be deprioritized based on the criteria you have set and scored. As an example, you may uncover that your consumer is a heavy Instagram user, but based on the prioritization criteria, Instagram is not the place you have chosen to invest for this initiative. Instead, the numbers have informed you to invest heavily on Facebook. In a scenario like this, you would most likely ignore Instagram, thereby creating a dead end experience. In Storyscaping, we would create some very lightweight content on Instagram that would link or point to Facebook. That way, consumers remain connected to the story and pass through the roundabout without getting lost.

**Town Centers.** These are the places where people congregate and where things happen—the centers of commerce. After you've gone though the process of scoring all possible touch points, you categorize them into lists of probable, likely, and optimal. The optimal touch points are the ones we tag as "town centers" because that is where the bulk of your resources should be focused when you are creating memorable and immersive experiences that sell. We will spend more time on describing "worlds that sell" in the next chapter.

**Destinations.** These are places of deep and valuable engagement that enable active participation. They are similar to town centers, except they don't have a form of transaction. The role here is to build on participation in an inspiring and immersed way, ultimately connecting to the town center through some form of system or content. An example of this is a game that you could play on a mobile device. It doesn't have an e-commerce platform in it for the products you sell, but it might reward you with offers to save and use when you visit the brand's website or store. A destination should always end in a comma and deeply engage. That engagement can be achieved through conversation, shared content, gaming, or other ways. The important part is that it must always connect to other destinations and/or town centers.

As we outlined previously, we include these tags in the spreadsheet for reference.

4. **Inspire:** We have effectively reimagined connections planning for a digitally disrupted world. The "build it and they will come" *Field of Dreams* promise comes to life when we uniquely apply story to this new breed of connections plan.

   At this stage of the game you have inventoried, prioritized, and tagged the Experience Space (your canvas) to ultimately address your business objectives. This is where your Organizing Idea comes into play. Take every one of those touch points you identified as the center of your brief. For example, if you are Coca-Cola and your Organizing Idea is "Open Happiness" and one of the key touch points is a vending machine, what big ideas could you and/or your team come up with? Now you can see the intersection and value of an Organizing Idea and how it meets up with a Story System.

And by understanding the role of the touch point (destination, town center, etc.), you are better equipped to build ideas and technologies that are connected, engaging, participatory, and relevant to your consumer. In action, you will find a new ability to consider ideas for their role in the Story System and not just an extension of an idea, or worse, a matching luggage adaptation of an idea.

You will also appreciate that this approach gives you amazing experiences at each touch point. Why? Because you have already defined the Organizing Idea, which relates to your consumers, and because you are not forcing ideas into channels. Instead, you are looking at channels as new opportunities. You will end with a different experience that is connected in story, in brand, and in experience. Wow, that's starting to sound like a Storyscape.

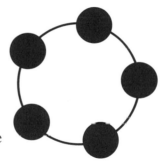

THE EXPERIENCE SPACE

5. **Optimize:** Whether or not you are religious, the King James Bible is a great example of a Story System. Depending on the size and type of book, a bible might be somewhere between 800 and 1,800 pages long. Very few people pick up the bible and read it in a linear manner from page 1 to page 1,800. The main reason for this is its structure. The bible is both a story and a series of stories—that's a Story System. For the über story delivered through the bible, its Organizing Idea could be described as something like "your personal

relationship with the beginning, middle, and end." We're not too religious, so we realize that may be rather general, but we're confident you get the point. You could literally open the bible to any page and discover a substory within the big story, which in itself has a plot, characters, setting, and narrative point of view. There is a moral to each story, and most notably, each of these substories or "experiences" serves the Organizing Idea.

It's very important to understand the distinction between Storyscaping and 360-degree marketing. In 360-degree marketing you effectively pummel the consumer with the same exact message or "matching luggage" from every angle. In a Story System like the bible, every story is not a different iteration of the same plot, it is its own story and it serves the bigger story.

**Connecting Story and System for Behavior.** The final step to explore is the unification of the story you tell, the content you produce, the experiences consumers have, and their participation with the brand. With ideas and stories in hand and an optimized Story System, we can more effectively consider the connection points between channels and touch points. You can consider this a process of inserting the commas in stories so they never end and inspire and facilitate connection to one another. Remember this important aspect in the definition of *Storyscape*, ". . . where each connection inspires engagement with another . . . " Now is the time to help facilitate and inspire that imperative aspect. We recognize that the consumer is in control of how they interact with the story. That's fundamental and will not change. As marketers, it is our job to inspire the journey and enable it where we can.

Start by looking at each idea and touch point and explore how it can connect with another, either in message or in system or both. At the most basic level, it could be a classic call to action such as "visit our website." Or it could be a solution you create using technology like the RFID chips in the EpicMix story that connects your personal profile and your pictures. We should always look for "commas" more like the latter of these two examples.

You can then explore more deeply by asking, "What is the motivation of consumers to engage with more of the story?" Go back to the consumer insights you have worked with and look at how they play out in creating and enabling these connections. As you start to think about the principle of connections and the motivations, you will be able to draw lines and connect the points for your Story System. These connections will produce a complete Storyscape, a world of immersive experiences, that inspire connection with each other and where the brand story becomes part of your consumer's story.

**System Teams for Teamed Systems.** Two quick notes on the series stages for Systems Thinking. First, it helps to create a collaboration team from multiple disciplines around this, which we detail in Chapter 12. Second, test and learn. Set up your approach and Story System so it is dynamic. Be flexible and prepare to start changing things. Be able to adapt to the performance variances, just like you might do with a call to action or with your landing pages from digital ads. It is quite common to do "test and learn" in a digital environment so that you maximize the value, but don't stop there. Think about how you can optimize the Story System at each and every point.

**Putting It All Together.** You are now well equipped with the basic concepts and tools on how to create an immersive Storyscape. Hopefully by reading these chapters, following along with our directions, and observing a sampling of our real-life examples, you have learned to not only recognize it but to harness its power by organizing through Systems Thinking and making sense of it all through story.

Those are the basics; and in the next chapter, we will explore how to build measurement plans, how to value the return on experience, and how to plan for the enabling technology platforms that will make your worlds sensing and adapting.

# WORLDS THAT SELL

*Constructing a Storyscape That Is Sensing and Adaptive*

# 11

# WORLDS THAT SELL

*Constructing a Storyscape That Is Sensing and Adaptive*

Whether you are an entrepreneur, a business owner, a marketer, or an agency type, at the end of the day, your role is to create perceptions and/or shift behaviors. These worlds we create must ultimately be tuned to driving commerce. This is projected by creating brand preference or simply building awareness, driving new customer acquisition, cross-selling products and services, focusing on client retention, and of course, encouraging fanatical customer advocacy.

**Building Worlds That Are Sensing.** The consumers' world—that of everyday experience—is an ecosystem rich in perceptions, attitudes, expectations, beliefs, interactions, actions, habits, and things. Business has only been able to capture, record, and measure a small (but useful) slice of that richness. We're changing that. We're changing that to enable dynamic application of marketing efforts through Storyscaping. As such, we will explore five perspectives for creating worlds that sell: instrumented ecosystems, adapting worlds, brand response, marketing mix optimization, and return on Storyscapes.

Typically we've leveraged survey data, point of sale data, purchase history, demographics, and very limited psychographics. We're now widening the aperture: converging new data sources and metrics from a broad range of consumer touch points, both physical and digital. We now have the ability to measure not only bits around people but now also places and things. We're changing the approach to Web-style analytics for the real world to provide actionable, "real-time," live labs, and real-world workbenches.

Today we learn much more by creating new, strategically significant, proprietary data sources from customers' interactions and experiences with things and places. As discussed in Chapter 8, we now employ sensors and other instruments that collect and process information in the real world in order to gain the most knowledge about consumer behavior today. This is in addition to the qualitative and quantitative data sources, which include social listening. This combination of research provides us with a much fuller picture. We can also build always-on, dynamic models of behaviors, interactions, contexts, and markets that are all wired with a robust ecosystem of analytic tools for making sense of it all.

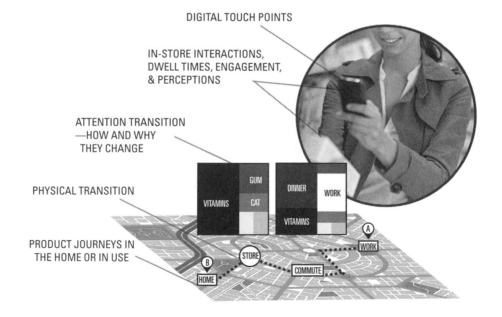

**Building Instrumented Ecosystems.** These days we can focus on long-term deployments of related sensors into contexts of everyday life or instrumented ecosystems. This provides a way of creating connected proprietary communities for the long-term development and evaluation of products, services, and communications. Sound complex? Observe the overlay of behavioral and mental models depicted earlier. These data points were easily obtained from a captive community of instrumented participants. Imagine if you had that kind of firsthand knowledge of how your customer gets through the day. Could this help you create better experiences, more relevant communications, or perhaps even more useful products and more effective Storyscapes? We believe it can and will.

**Building Worlds That Are Adapting.** There are two dimensions to this notion of adapting worlds. The first is adapting a set of experiences to more efficiently yield a behavior such as "get more people to buy." The second is adapting a set of experiences to make a more memorable experience. In Storyscaping, you need to do both effectively, and sometimes they are at odds with each other. Here is a simple story and example we use to teach Web designers how to think about this conflict. We'll start in with a question: "Have you ever heard the story where Walt Disney walks up to one of the groundskeepers shortly after the opening of Disneyland and says, "I've seen you out here all week. Why do you keep having to replant these flowers?" The groundskeeper responds, "Sir, the guests keep ruining this particular flowerbed; they're using it as a shortcut to get to the concession stand—but don't worry sir, I'm going to build a white picket fence around it." To this Walt responded, "Forget the fence; pave the path." Although we are not quite sure if that actually happened that way, we use it as a good example of user-centered design thinking. The challenge we find is that this line of thinking is about "enabling natural behaviors" as opposed to "shifting or manipulating" behaviors. We feel it's much more difficult to get someone to do something they were not already planning to do and then feel good about the experience.

That was the story, and here is the real-world example we use to demonstrate the pitfalls. Let's explore an online credit card application. If you took 100 Web designers, information architects, and user-experience designers, 90 percent of them would tell you that a one-step, one-page application, with the least number of questions possible, provides the "best experience." If you were to ask 100 consumers the same question, they would agree completely. The facts, however, tell a different tale. The performance facts say that a three-step application is optimal and even a five-step application will convert a higher number of prospects from start to finish, ultimately ending in the prospect applying for an account. The behavioral insight is that asking for a social security number is a "deal breaker" question—people get nervous and abandon the process. That said, if the progress bar shows you are on step three of three, then you are "invested" and are therefore more likely to press the "Submit" button; this translates into many more new customers. If it's difficult to get professional Web designers to make that connection to performance marketing, then ask yourself if this pitfall could be happening in your organization. Is the team who is running your digital properties focused on "usability" or sales?

The second dimension is that we can perform multivariate testing for creative, offer, placement, time, and you name it. Behavioral targeting, day parting, personalization should not be relegated to "search" and "digital display" marketing. The physical and virtual worlds and the technologies that measure and move content and provide servicing and support are all being connected. Imagine all of the window displays at various stores in the mall. Why couldn't we measure and optimize how well each of them drives sales? Digital displays are not necessary. The same old posters and mannequins that exist there today would still work. With a few cameras and some cheap software, we could track just how many people walk in front of each store (impressions) and we could anonymously assess whether they are male or female and provide an approximate age. We could observe whether they are a solo visitor or if they arrived in various packs. We could easily measure if they stop and linger in front of the window (engagement), and of course, we could tell if they went into the store. With a bit more work and investment, we could even confirm whether they made a purchase and we could calculate the average check. All of this is possible. Now, if we did have those digital displays, we could also serve content to them—imagine the possibilities. We could customize the windows to promote the excess inventory that our system reports confirm we have sitting in the back storage area. We could test creative. We could optimize to average check. We could enhance the dwell experience by providing more content if someone stops to look at the display. How many opportunities are out there like this for your business?

Technologists should never be relegated to just building the platforms that measure or enable what creatives conjure up. They must be part of the creative team that is imagining what's possible. Gathering data is one thing, but using real-time data as actionable insights and triggers for optimizing your return and enhancing the experience often through technology is what Storyscaping is all about.

**A World of Brand Response.** Are you a "brand-centered" or "response-centered" marketer? Over the years, we've observed that clients big and small, old or new, tend to lean one way or the other, but seldom, and we mean very seldom, do we find a marketer who truly breaks those boundaries and connects both of those two worlds. We believe this type of connected thinking breeds the best kind of marketer. When asked this question, most people immediately jump to say they are one of those chosen few that embrace both worlds and we will always challenge that. Understanding and appreciating the differences between brand and direct marketing is one thing, but truly understanding the interdependencies between the two is different. It's like being left- or right-handed; people favor one over the other. In this new Storyscaping world, the real opportunity lies in this connection. Today someone can become aware of a product, research it further, and purchase that product on his or her smartphone—all within a few minutes. We've come to know that there is more than just brand marketing and direct response; there is some great gooey stuff in the middle. We call this Brand Response.

Breaking down boundaries between brand marketing thinking and direct response thinking is just the beginning. Additionally, there is a very obvious relationship and a clear balance that must be managed between demand generation, demand harvesting and demand satisfaction. Storyscaping requires

## WORLDS THAT LINK COMMUNICATIONS TO COMMERCE

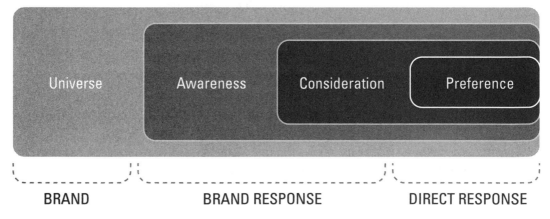

a ton of boundary breaking. There are lots of collaborations and cross-channel and discipline connections that need to be made. Because so many businesses are already finding themselves facing an increasingly interconnected set of big strategic questions that need to be answered, we suggest that you proactively choose to blur these boundaries.

We have come to a point in time when the value created by connections can overshadow any core capability. Consider this a bit further. Can you create great communications without understanding the role of experience, leveraging the insights derived from analytics, and harnessing the power of technology? Can you create a great immersive experience without leveraging the power of story or having some level of mastery on enabling technologies? Consumers move seamlessly through physical and virtual spaces and emotional states. Therefore, you need to as well. This takes a new and evolved set of skills.

**Media Mix Modeling versus Marketing Mix Optimization.** In the previous chapter, we discussed the basic need to take inventory and then prioritize touch points according to your business objectives. We uncovered the need to avoid media myopia and instead operate with a broader aperture. At the most basic level, this holds true even if you have the means and can employ advanced modeling techniques. Avoid putting too much focus on *media mix* alone and step up to *marketing mix* intelligence. There are real challenges facing legacy solutions for media mix, such as relying on swim lane analytics. If you follow this path, you will continue struggling to capture cross-media effects and thus make it impossible to quantify how offline and online work together. Without comparable and consistent metrics, you will never get a true and holistic view of the marketplace and your insight generation will crawl along very slowly.

Advancements in marketing mix modeling can answer certain questions for us: How does social and nontraditional marketing amplify other channels? What are the marketing efficiencies across the portfolio of channels and initiatives? What is your return on investment (or value) driven from nontraditional marketing? Because this information is actually modeled across channels, it offers a true, holistic view of the results. In addition to the direct impact on sales, we can also evaluate the interconnectivity of the entire Experience Space. This includes the paid, owned, and earned within digital media and holistically across all media channels. When you can clearly see, understand, and compare these impacts, you will never again underestimate how the removal of one channel influences all of the channels. This leads to more effective and efficient decision making.

**Measuring Return on Storyscapes.** Throughout this book, we have shared stories and insight into the fact that the digital revolution ushered in the information age, and along with it came a huge number of changes in the

**MACRO**                                             **MICRO**

**WIDE-ANGLE VIEW MARKETING MIX**

Understand own and competitive performance. Quantify own ROI and performance by key tactic.

**CROSS-CHANNEL ATTRIBUTION**

Understand how activation on one mix elements impacts another quantify-attributed versus nonattributed ROI

**DIGITAL ATTRIBUTION**

Drill down into digital and understand conversion path rates, placement, and optimal frequency way we all experience everyday life. This shift and its respective consequences continues unabated because of the ever-expanding array of electronic and digital technologies, which bring us computing and communication tools such as smartphones, tablets, social media, and almost everything we can imagine. All of these continue to contribute to our ability to have whole new forms of interaction, activity, and expectations.

For those of us in the business of marketing and the marketing of business, the digital revolution is also forcing upon us a reexamination of underlying assumptions and models for how brands connect with customers and, most important, how we measure and value that. We have also explained that the long-held assumption that companies unilaterally control their brand and that consumers are merely recipients of our well-crafted corporate messages is no longer valid. The balance of control has shifted to consumers who have extremely high expectations. This is creating the need for more sophisticated ways of shaping their expectations and experiences and, more important, better ways to gauge their efforts in doing so.

The upshot for marketing is that we are moving from a push-driven traditional brand-centric view of the world to an experience and engagement economy for connected experiences that are co-owned by brand and consumer. Therefore, we must also re imagine how we measure the value of investments.

There is also a fascinating and ongoing debate about the role of technology (media and the channels themselves) and how it has become a shaping force in the practice of marketing. Some argue that marketing-related technologies (TV, radio, or other mass media/channels) have largely dictated how marketing, including products and brands of all shapes and sizes, operates as it does today. Decades of practice have led inexorably toward conclusions about how the constituent parts of the company-customer link (brand, product, message, company, media, receiver, audience, etc.) relate to one another. Over time, launching ads through mass media and mass channels has become a *method* of working. This underlying model can be characterized through the notion of a sender, a channel, and a receiver, totaling a process of *pushing* messages toward consumers. In this model, consumers are assumed to be mere recipients of a product or brand story and are exemplified as "eyeballs," "targets," and "audiences" that must be penetrated and then measured by recall, impressions, and mindshare. This method has proved effective in cases where the story comes alive, appears clever, sticks, or gets retold; the brand gets stronger and the company gains a new customer.

As we explore more of the consumer and brand connection in the Experience Space, two limits to this historical approach have come into sharp relief. The first is a limit in the media itself. We haven't historically understood much about what is actually going on out there after the push. It's a launch-and-leave world where companies only have a surface-level knowledge of their customer's story. In some sense, we didn't need to know more than that; the thinnest possible report from the field sufficed by answering the basics: How many consumer targets increased awareness of the brand? How many prospects became customers?

Yet, even if companies want to know more about what happened after the push, they couldn't learn much because it was limited by the nature of the media. What can be known in a push world of static media and channels? With the shift toward an always-on consumer who is connected in new ways, both socially and digitally, companies need to develop new ways to connect to their customers now more than ever.

The second limit is the implicit assumption that people are simple, passive recipients of messages. They are no such thing. They are *willing participants* in a world of experience with your brand, products, and services. People are using the things companies make and sell to tell stories to one another about who they are. And in that telling, people get other ideas, they discover new things to do and new ways to be who they are, and they are always looking for ways to make those stories new, better, and more compelling. This is why we need to understand them, their frames of reference, and their language.

## BEYOND PUSH AND PULL

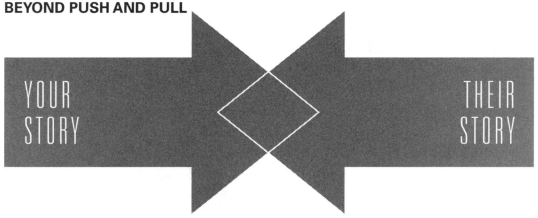

SYMMETRICAL—OWNED BY COMPANY AND CUSTOMER

| HOW | EVALUATE AND MEASURE | GOAL |
|---|---|---|
| Engagement platforms + Organizing Idea Company as story enabler, extender. Company creates the conditions for experience. Persistent, viral, always-on. | The experiences of people, places, and things; interactions; and perceptions. | Connect with consumers. Be relevant & meaningful. |

**Measuring—Is It the New Black?** We have introduced a measurement model that recognizes the new reality of commerce and marketing. It was created by building onto old models that still work, and then adding a new way to think about, optimize, and measure the value of experiences—the overall return of an investment in building a Storyscape.

This shift in the ways we can connect brands and consumers through Storyscaping requires a parallel shift, one that offers new and better ways to instrument, measure, and model these connections. Having these helps paint a more accurate picture of people's actual experience.

## MEASURING RETURN IN THE NEW ERA

We must measure marketing effect outside of traditional advertising and sales channels, and take on a broader and more inclusive definition of marketing itself.

And revenue.

This type of execution, which is cocreated, data-rich, and deeply motivational, requires new kinds of descriptive and prescriptive tools.

① Yields aggregate business ROI

**BRAND & MARKETING ROI**

**RETURN ON MEDIA & CHANNELS**

**EXPERIENCE OPTIMIZATION**

② Measure consumer engagement within channels themselves

③ Quantitative and qualitative techniques for optimizing consumer experience

The model to the left shows how business creates value across connected experiences and how that value can be followed and measured into individual moments. It is composed of three parts:

1. Aggregate measures to assess the return on storytelling and experience initiatives
2. Next-generation marketing mix and cross-media analytics to provide a more detailed and accurate picture of channel effect
3. Experience measurement framework to more precisely assess experience with a new frame of reference and new measurement tools, such as sensor technology, that produce new forms of consumer behavior data at a level that can be mined for insights.

**Brand and Marketing ROI.** First, let's discuss the return on investment (ROI) of brand and marketing, which is a variety of business analytics used to evaluate return and efficiencies at the aggregate level. These are classic measures, such as ROI analyses, market share, cost/benefit, or balanced scorecard.

Nike tells a compelling story in the aggregate. In the past three years, Nike's print and ad spend has decreased 40 percent, while their overall annual marketing budget has increased to $2.4 billion[1] (CNN Money, February 12, 2012). Where are the Nike dollars going? The money funds the building of ecosystems where customers can experience products, digital environments, apps, and websites. Stefan Olander, vice president of digital sport at Nike, explains this shift in spending: "When you have millions of people that come back and reconnect with your brand multiple times a week, you realize that that connection is more valuable and powerful than any traditionally pushed marketing message."[2] He's talking about the value of the Nike experience.  If you can get a customer to continue engaging

213

with your brand multiple times a week, the effects soar beyond any traditional marketing campaign.

Using our model, you can see the bigger picture. Nike wasn't getting enough return out of their media spend, so it shifted it to a bigger spend on experience. This improved the return on media and channels, making everything more efficient. Raising the return on experience (RoX) gave that spend greater legs, resulting in a maximized ROI.

Olander also stated, "The biggest audience Nike had on any given day was when 200 million tuned into the Super Bowl. Now, across all its sites and social media communities, it can hit that figure any given day."[3]

**Return on Media and Channels**. The second element of our model addresses return on media and channels. Recent developments in the field of media mix modeling use sophisticated next generation algorithms (mathematical models) to quantify cross-media effects of marketing.

Traditionally, media mix modeling measures a given channel's direct effect on sales. Yet, if we apply new era thinking to this scenario, thinking that comprehends how experience connects media, a flaw in the traditional thinking is revealed. During an average day, there are perhaps several hundred touch points living across a huge variety of media and channels, none of which, by the way, happen with people who think they are having a multichannel experience; they are simply going about the day, living out their story.

There is a need for a new media measurement model that effectively optimizes across channels and stays consistent with how people actually live. Through capabilities, such as (m)PHASIZE's (a SapientNitro company) marketing mix modeling tools, we can bring to bear custom-built, proprietary analytics tools and services that help marketing executives make optimal budget allocation and planning decisions based on they way people move and respond throughout their days and across their ecosystem. Innovative predictive forecasting models enable you to run what-if scenarios that simulate how targeted consumers will respond to different variables. This offers an ability to quantify cross-channel impacts while taking into account the interplay between traditional media (radio, print, TV) and digital (search, display, social, mobile) at a brand and category level. This wide-angle approach enables clients to continuously measure and calibrate marketing investments to generate incremental ROI in today's dynamic, always-on marketplace.

**Experience Optimization.** Advanced media analytics propel us a little further into consumer engagement with media and channels, but still provide no insight into actions *within* channels or *with* media. Optimizing a budget around media and channels only to draw people to a place where they will have a mediocre experience is a waste of efforts and a missed opportunity.

Therefore, we extend our capabilities to measure experience and optimize how we build for it. Again, Nike's Stefan Olander provides an excellent example that illustrates the value of understanding the other: "We don't start with technology or the potential profit, we always start with the athlete. I think that's an important distinction, because when you do that, the other things follow."[4]

The current means for assessing experience don't do justice to the nuance and range of how people act, connect with others, or sense (and make sense of) their world. For starters, there is a need for better sources of data and ways to harvest it. In the era of big data, there exists a deluge of inputs, but volumes of data alone do not tell the story. Complementary and comprehensive data is needed, not only on how people behave (of which there are many sources), but also from data collected from the objects they use and the environments they inhabit over time.

As discussed and illustrated in some Chapter 8 stories, everyday consumer products—homes, offices, retail spaces, civil infrastructure, and even the natural environment—all have the capacity to communicate. With applied technology through sensors, they deliver huge volumes of real-time data at a level of detail never before possible. These data can be used alone or correlated with other quantitative or qualitative sources to deliver a powerful new kind of business intelligence, thus turning these new information pathways into real business value. Greater depth and detail is reached, and it changes as the world and people change. Granular data, combined with advanced analytics and visualization techniques, make for better, faster, cheaper data upon which we can ultimately build connections between brands and customers.

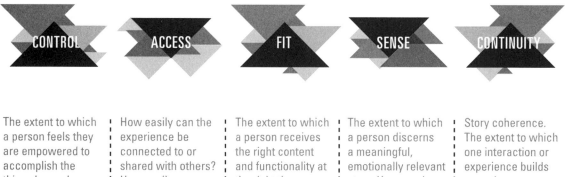

| CONTROL | ACCESS | FIT | SENSE | CONTINUITY |
|---|---|---|---|---|
| The extent to which a person feels they are empowered to accomplish the things he or she wants or needs to do. How well does the Storyscape support user goals or tasks? | How easily can the experience be connected to or shared with others? How easily can you become part of, or affect, the story? | The extent to which a person receives the right content and functionality at the right time. | The extent to which a person discerns a meaningful, emotionally relevant story. How much does the experience leave an impression or expression? | Story coherence. The extent to which one interaction or experience builds upon the next. |

To more precisely measure the dimensions of experience in this step, we developed a new model of experience.  It was originally developed for urban planning by Kevin Lynch in *Good City Form*[5] and then modified by our teams for use within brand strategy and experience design. We've identified five experience dimensions that are used to assess how well a particular campaign, design, interaction, or environment, performs in terms of experience. These dimensions include control, access, fit, sense, and continuity.

These experience dimensions form the core of the experience assessment used in our approach to experience design and strategy.

**Return in the New Era of Marketing.**  Many of yesterday's and even today's marketing and branding efforts seek empathic messages that resonate with consumers' stories. But even the best of these, pushed through static channels, won't meet the requirements of engagement and participation that people expect. "Engagement" is a mantra that must be chanted, recited, and repeated throughout all dimensions of business execution—from products, messages, services, and environments to media, channels, and eventually toward topline business results.

It's vital to have a comprehensive picture of the consumer as a person. The old view of people as objects of commerce provides a very limited understanding, and it tells only a fraction of the full story. We must leverage the power of information technologies and the "digital exhaust" they produce in order to dig more deeply into their story. The goal is to mine these realities, use them to fuel creative execution, and to inform the dynamic application of Systems Thinking for the most effective worlds of experience.

We appreciate that mastering these five perspectives is no walk in the park. It takes diverse skill sets and capabilities. It also takes a certain spirit and culture to inspire these necessary, changed perspectives and fuel adoption. In other words, you need to shock your culture.

# SHOCK YOUR CULTURE

*Creating an Environment That Is Conducive*
*to Great Storyscaping*

# SHOCK YOUR CULTURE

*Creating an Environment That Is Conducive*
*to Great Storyscaping*

We've reached the final chapter, and we hope you will find it to be the most important. At this point along the journey, you have been armed with an evolved perspective on how combining a great narrative, immersive experiences, and lots of Systems Thinking can create incredible success for your business. We believe that with this knowledge and an open mind, you can tackle your marketing using the Storyscaping mind-set and a more modern approach. Whether you are just getting started or consider yourself to be a seasoned veteran, and regardless of the resources at your disposal, we are convinced this philosophy and the simple model we have provided will help you achieve better outcomes. That's the easy part.

In our view, the hard part, which is always the hardest part when you are dealing with a people-based business, is the people side of the equation. So it's now time to shock your culture. How? Let us share some broad thoughts and a few things about our culture that you might consider for yours.

**Collaboration of Connection.** Collaboration is an easy concept for anyone to grasp, but it's very difficult to actually do in any organization. Small organizations are not immune to the challenges that stem from ego and personal insecurity. Yes, you can reasonably expect that the bigger and more hierarchical your company gets, the harder it becomes to harness real collaboration. *Culture* and *environment* are the ultimate answers. The ultimate secret weapon lies within your ability to imagine, develop, and foster a culture and environment conducive to Storyscaping.

We truly believe that there are two manifestations of functional cultures that help companies grow. The rest are dysfunctional in the sense that their limitations far exceed their benefits. The first functional model for corporate culture is one that depends on shared values, shared goals, and shared perspectives. This is a culture of "sameness" where teamwork, focus and camaraderie are the intangible benefits. The second functional model is one that depends heavily on a shared Purpose and embraces diversity of skills and perspectives. This is not at all about sameness; instead, it's about alignment to a cause or belief. The latter is what is required to effectively drive Storyscaping.

Ask yourself this question. In the event you or one of your loved ones became very ill, would you rather have five doctors all from different fields of science and medicine working as a collaborative team to diagnose the problem and find the best cure, or would you prefer to have five similar doctors, each with the same perspective and experience, who all come from the same field of medicine, trying to figure out what could possibly be wrong? Well, we would take option one every time because we believe in the power of "connected thinking." We don't believe in the lone genius. The goal of our collaboration is to make connections between ideas and people and people and behaviors and then test the strength of those new connections to make sure they'll hold. Let us repeat—we believe in the power of "connected thinking." Our strategists, planners, technologists, writers, and art directors are brilliant in their own fields, but we nearly always find the best ideas come up during the dialogue between people from different disciplines. An idea's richness and depth percolates when strategists and designers hash things out together, when writers and technologists share left and right-brained thoughts, and when thinkers and doers are both "all-in" throughout the entire project. This collaboration brings to life insights that could go untapped when people are left in their own rooms, mining the blank page for gold. An application of connected thinking moves random ideas toward creative solutions.

**True Collaboration versus Subservient Corporate Structures.** Can you truly be collaborative in an environment where goals and incentives are focused or interpreted primarily around individual performance and career progression? Does the most tenured person in the room always get the last say on who has the best idea? Does that really foster innovation or progression? This is really a sensitive and tricky territory. In the agency world there tends to always be someone at the helm who ultimately has the last say on what ideas are pursued and which ones hit the cutting room floor. Those self-proclaimed geniuses tend to come in two flavors. In our opinion, the best ones are more like benevolent dictators; they do a great job of listening; they are great at including others and great at building very dedicated and loyal teams. This works very effectively, but because so much hinges on the strengths and sensibilities of the leader, it does not scale well. The other flavor of leader is more of a megalomaniac who always has to have the last say and believes no idea is a great idea unless it comes from them. Unfortunately this is very prevalent in our industry. We have good news—there is an alternative.

At Sapient, our roots were grounded in more of a consulting company model. This means our assignment teams have been dynamically assembled based on the client ask. When our assignment was to develop a strategy to launch a product in a new market, we assembled a team of experts who were appropriate for the project. After the assignment was complete, each of those experts would have likely been redeployed to another assignment where they would be paired up with a whole different set of team members. This application of multidiscipline dynamic team-building serves connected thinking well. Today we operate in both consulting and agency modes so that we can leverage this

DNA to fuel our collaboration and negate any instances of megalomania or dictatorial behavior.

**Not One of Us Is Smarter Than All of Us**. Designing your team is, in and of itself, a craft. The time and attention required for this aspect of your culture recipe is equally important to the others, yet its soundness is most often underestimated. That is why we dedicated a whole chapter on sharing what works to culminate the best of your specialized resources—the people and the team. The best examples we can provide for this chapter come from our living outline of how we've managed to shock our own culture within SapientNitro. Our company started with six core values in mind that have shaped and guided every choice we've made: Openness, Relationships, People growth, Leadership, Client focus and Creativity. Think about how some of those same values may make perfect sense in your organization. Think of your entire staff as a collection of creative-minded individuals who are all collaborating to solve problems and make an impact on people's lives. We believe that in order to make anything happen, you need these creative-minded people to play three critical roles: the architect, the steward, and the craftsperson. Each playing their part as the need arises but never limiting themselves to one single role as the project needs evolve. We call this "Idea Engineering."

**Architecture.** In the same way that Joseph Beuys said, "Everyone is an artist,"[1] we believe that everyone is creative. In our world, the project managers, account directors, social media junkies, ethnographers, technologists, media planners, strategists, designers, and copywriters each contribute to the creative process that brings great ideas to life.

So to us, it's less about "being creative" or "doing creative" things and more about the application of creativity, not serendipitously, but consistently from region to region, office to office, and team to team. This does not mean we don't believe in big ideas. Rather, we firmly believe that ideas of all sizes and shapes have little value unless you bring them to life. After all, it's only the great ideas that we bring to life that empower human potential and change the world.

For people who come from the world of advertising, it's hard to imagine that at one time the copywriters and the art directors worked on different floors of their respective buildings and never interacted. We now know the magic of how an art director and copywriter encourage each other to think of their assignments in new ways. With this shift, each became more committed to the quality of the work, because neither could simply hand off their work to someone else at the end. Many "creative" companies today still continue on day after day, quarter after quarter without admitting to themselves that it's unwise to separate departments in this new interconnected world. In many places, technologists still sit on different floors of their buildings than where the writers sit, as do the art directors. Planners and strategists are sealed away in strategy departments. At SapientNitro, we could not imagine a world where technologists, creatives, and strategists don't work hand in hand. When we brainstorm, three is hardly a crowd, and often four, five, or six is even better. Our "collective" informs our culture, showing the way for what's possible and what's next. The goal is to put the right talent on the right problem.

Sure, there have been the occasional fortunate accidents and incremental adjustments to an existing idea, but most of the major leaps that are made are in response to some threat, obstacle, or problem to be solved. And the best solutions come from asking the right questions. This is often called "the wisdom of babes," and it's the kind of wisdom that leads us to question our assumptions and look at our world with greater attention. It rewrites the instruction manual instead of abandoning the dream. It redesigns the packaging when we thought we were fishing for a new campaign. It launches a nationwide bus tour when all that happened around this time last year was an e-mail blast.

> *"Nothing worked. So then I thought I'd try the wrong shape, and it worked."*
>
> —James Dyson[2]

James Dyson's vacuum cleaner sucked, and sucked badly, so badly that he was motivated to invent a new one. It took 15 years and exactly 5,126 failed prototypes before he hit gold by doing it "wrong." Dyson finally created a better vacuum once he abandoned the established and expected rules. In his own words, "I started out trying a conventionally shaped cyclone, but we couldn't separate the carpet fluff and dog hairs and strands of cotton in those cyclones. I tried all sorts of shapes. Nothing worked. So then I thought I'd try the wrong shape, the opposite of (the traditional) conical. And it worked." How did his strategic approach work? His "wrong thinking" worked so well that the titans of the industry balked at his new design and refused to buy his invention, believing they had the right way, and no other way existed. So Dyson was forced to go at it alone, and barely squeaked by selling slightly more than 15 million units, some retailing for as much as $2,000 to date.

> *"Sometimes the questions are complicated and the answers are simple."*
>
> — Dr. Seuss[3]

Success is yours for the asking. The need to question everything in business is the reason "what if . . . ?" people, "how can we . . . ?" people and "why . . . ?" people exist—to make sure the real problem is being addressed. Asking the right questions, or failing to do so, has changed industries from railroading to movie rentals. Imagine for a second that the companies that started the movie rental industry had initially invested in the Internet and provided their subscribers access to DVDs without having to travel to and enter a store with limited supply. What if the railroad industry recognized that they were, above all else, actually in the transportation business and decided to boost their offerings by investing in airlines? The power behind asking the right question is that it reveals the right path for us and for our clients.

**Stewardship.** Creativity is a fragile, volatile, and collaborative journey that needs equal parts stewardship and imagination. The role of stewardship should never be undervalued. For Michelangelo, it was the Pope; for Vincent Van Gogh, it was his brother Theo; for Michael Jordan, it was either Phil Jackson or Nike, depending on who you ask. The most dedicated stewards figure out the real goal behind a request, involve stakeholders, and keep everyone engaged and collaborating. They protect infant ideas, providing them the time, space, and nurturing needed to grow into healthy, wise, and perfectly ripe ideas. They also understand how an idea solves the key problem and are able to advocate on behalf of the best possible solution. This start-to-finish ownership is a responsibility for everyone in the company, and is a prerequisite to delivering a successful solution.

**Craft.** We celebrate the power of craftsmanship, and the way we approach it is a way in which few companies in any industry can copy. Technologists, programmers, usability experts, and media professionals lead the charge by building the most breakthrough solutions. It's not enough to have a great idea if it never sees the light of day. The skilled craftsperson collaborates with other stakeholders to make sure that great idea is perfectly executed. Together, they become a team where each teammate is equally passionate about craft. They troubleshoot and test so that every creation offers the end user an experience that makes a difference in that person's day and life.

These three critical roles of architect, steward, and craftsperson often manifest daily in the way that everyone goes about their job. The combination of these ingredients is the foundation for realizing an idea, and it nestles in at the heart of Storyscaping.

The fact that technology has been changing all of our lives at a breathtaking pace makes this a great time to be creative. And we as business owners, decision makers, and game changers are right in the center of that thrilling change every day. Fortunately, the speed of change hasn't tempered humanity's fascination with and impulse toward creativity—it's actually fuelled it. So it's critical to have a spirit to solve as well as a spirit to create.

Back in the day, Carroll Shelby and his team of California hot rod engineers (with support from Henry Ford) displayed a foxhole mentality and a can-do spirit as they hand-built their car, the Cobra. In their day, they challenged and beat Ferrari, shaking up the racing world. There was a steward in Henry Ford and architects and craftspeople in Shelby's team.[4] It was a combination of creativity applied for solutions. That team, their mentality, and their spirit are an example of what Idea Engineering represents at SapientNitro. In the same way that these folks did, we are taking on the establishment by proving you don't need a well-known brand or 50 years of legacy to create something that accelerates progress and usurps the position of the lead dog. What you need is a committed and diverse team, some ingenuity, and the willingness to retool when an engine or two blows up in your face. Having a spirit that makes an impact on the world by bringing ideas to life is why we are constantly working to craft the next great Organizing Idea, the next big solution, the next inspiring story, and most assuredly, the next world of immersive experiences. It's also why we then seek to surpass it.

We sincerely hope that sharing a little of our approach to culture and creativity will inspire you to reflect on what it will take to empower Storyscaping within your organization. Remember, we know through experience that the functional model required to effectively drive Storyscaping depends heavily on a shared Purpose and embraces diversity of skills and perspectives. Are you ready to shock your culture?

In closing, we reflect on our journey of Storyscaping. We opened with the value of stories and how we use them to create meaning in our lives, highlighting the fact that stories help us understand the workings and threads of the world. Next, we explored the unsung hero known as "experience," and put a spotlight on the value of bringing stories and experience together. Then, the Storyscaping model was introduced and the many dimensions of brands and consumers were explored at length. We defined and illustrated Organizing Ideas, the Experience Space, Systems Thinking, and Story Systems so they can become a welcomed part of your marketing team, too. Last, we lifted the veil on organizational culture, showcasing collaboration and connected thinking as the showstoppers that fuel Storyscaping.

We hope this journey has helped you imagine a new way of working that fits the new world we all live in. We are confident that many of the thoughts and tips we shared throughout this book will invoke a spark that enables your potential (both brand and company) to grow and develop beyond where you previously imagined. Above all, we hope that this story becomes part of your story.

# REFERENCES

# REFERENCES

## INTRODUCTION

1. Rocket Silverman, Justin, "Invasion of the Cabbage Patchers," *New York Times,* September 10, 2008.

2. Kane, Colleen, "Cabbage Patch Fever: 25 Years After," *Huffington Post,* December 19, 2008, http://www.huffingtonpost.com/colleen-kane/cabbage-patch-fever-25ye_b_152470.html

3. "What Makes Your Brand Unique?" Build-A-Bear Corporate Website, Frequently Asked Questions 5, accessed October 24, 2013, http://www.buildabear.com/shopping/contents/content.jsp?id=2300007.

4. "What's the Most Popular Animal?" Build-A-Bear Corporate Website, Frequently Asked Questions 7, accessed October 24, 2013, http://www.buildabear.com/shopping/contents/content.jsp?id=2300007.

5. "A History of Helping Girls Shine," American Girl Corporate Website, Company History, accessed October 24, 2013, http://www.americangirl.com/corp/corporate.php?section=about&id=2.

6. Alva, Marilyn, "Mattel Shares Rise on Profits, American Girl Sales," *Investor's Business Daily,* accessed October 24, 2013, http://news.investors.com/.business/041713–652230-mattel-beats-hasbro-to-report-financial-results.htm.

7. "Fast Facts," American Girl Corporate Website, accessed October 24, 2013, http://www.americangirl.com/corp/corporate.php?section=about&id=6.

## 01  FROM THE CAMPFIRE

1. Amos, Jonathan, "Red Dot Becomes 'Oldest Cave Art,'" *BBC News,* June 14, 2012, http://www.bbc.co.uk/news/science-environment-18449711.

2. Choi, Charles, "Hot Find! Humans Used Fire 1 Million Years Ago," Livescience.com, April 2012, accessed October 24, 2013, http://www.livescience.com/19425-earliest-human-fire.html.

3. Booker, Christopher. *The Seven Basic Plots: Why We Tell Stories.* New York: Continuum, 2004.

4. Campbell, Joseph. *The Hero's Journey: The World of Joseph Campbell: Joseph Campbell on His Life and Work*. San Francisco: Harper & Row, 1960.

5. "Our Movement—Giving Shoes & Sight," TOMS Corporate Website, accessed October 2013, http://www.toms.com/our-movement/l.

6. "What is J.K. Rowling's Involvement in This Project?" Universal Orlando Corporate Website, Harry Potter World FAQs, accessed October 2013, https://www.universalorlando.com/Theme-Parks/Islands-of-Adventure/Wizarding-World-of-Harry-Potter/FAQ.aspx.

7. Mildenhall, Jonathan, Senior Vice President Integrated Marketing Content and Design Excellence, The Coca-Cola Company. Interviewed by Gaston Legorburu & Darren McColl. Atlanta, GA. August 16, 2013.

8. "Unilever Sustainable Living Plan: Our Company Strategy." Unilever Progress Report 2012. Page 4. Accessed October 28, 2013. http://www.unilever.com/images/USLP-Progress-Report-2012-FI_tcm13-352007.pdf.

9. "Company Overview," Google.com. Accessed November 20, 2013. http://www.google.com/about/company/.

10. Dugdale, Addy, "Adidas May Be Official World Cup Sponsor, but Nike Wins the Battle of the Buzz," *Fast Company,* June 2010, accessed October 2013, http://www.fastcompany.com/1658906/adidas-may-be-official-world-cup-sponsor-nike-wins-battle-buzz.

## 02  YOUR FIRST KISS

1. Shayon, Sheila, "Disgruntled British Airways Passenger Airs Out Grievance through Promoted Tweet," BrandChannel, September 3, 2013, accessed October 2013, http://www.brandchannel.com/home/post/British-Airways-Passenger-Promoted-Tweet-090313.aspx.

2. "Company Overview," Waltdisney.com. 2013. http://thewaltdisneycompany.com/about-disney/company-overview.

3.  Lev, Michael, "Hanna-Barbera Follows Disney Map," *New York Times,* January 1990, accessed October 2013, http://www.nytimes.com/1990/01/09 /business/hanna-barbera-follows-disney-map.html?src=pm.

4.  "Innovations: We Don't Just Make Car. We Design the Ultimate Driving Machine," BMW Corporate Website, accessed October 2013, http://www .bmwusa.com/standard/content/innovations/default.aspx.

## 03  BRAVE NEW WORLDS

1.  Tolle, Eckhart, *A New Earth: Awakening to Your Life's Purpose.* New York: Dutton/Penguin Group, 2005.

2.  "Eckhart Tolle," Oprah Corporate Website, Oprah Radio Webcasts, July 10, 2008, http://www.oprah.com/oprahradio/Eckhart-Tolle-on-Oprahs-Soul-Series -Webcast.

3.  Jensen, Jeff, "Great Expectations." *Entertainment Weekly*. January 24, 2007. Accessed Nov 21, 2013.

4.  Cassidy, Anne, "Good Characters and Cool Stuff—James Cameron on the Evolution of Storytelling." Co.Create. *Fast Company*. June 3, 2013. Accessed November 21, 2013. http://www.fastcocreate.com/1683090/good-characters -and-cool-stuff-james-cameron-on-the-evolution-of-storytelling.

5.  Marsh, Ed W., *James Cameron's Titanic.* London: Boxtree, 1998, 3–29.

6.  "James Cameron," OceanElders.org, accessed October 28, 2013, http://www .oceanelders.org/elder/james-cameron.

7.  "New Performance Capture Technology Video," Science.discovery.com: Science Channel, Discovery Communications. http://science.discovery.com /video-topics/sci-fi-supernatural/james-cameron-interview-new-performance -capture-technology.htm.

8.  "Avatar: Science Behind Pandora Video." Discovery Channel.com, Discovery Channel. December 22, 2010. Accessed November 1, 2013." http://news .discovery.com/tech/videos/tech-avatar-science-behind-pandora.htm.

9. Thompson, Anne, "How James Cameron's Innovative New 3D Tech Created Avatar." *Popular Mechanics*, January 1, 2010. Accessed November 21, 2013. http://www.popularmechanics.com/technology /digital/visual-effects/4339455.

10. "Vail Resorts Announces Launch Schedule of EpicMix™ and Epic Holiday Gift Contest." Investors.VailResorts.com, November 2010, accessed October 28, 2013, http://investors.vailresorts.com/releasedetail .cfm?releaseid=526910.

11. "Lindsey Vonn Race Series," EpicMix.com, accessed October 28, 2013, http:// www.epicmix.com/lindsey-vonn-race-series.aspx.

## 04 THE STORYSCAPING MODEL

1. Gourevitch, Peter, "A New Model of Corporate Social Responsibility: A Case Study of TOMS Shoes," School of International Relations and Pacific Studies, UC San Diego, Irps.ucsd.edu, Winter 2012, accessed October 28, 2013, http:// irps.ucsd.edu/assets/001/503681.pdf.

## 05 POWER OF WHY

1. Lukovits, Karlene, "Fastest-Growing Brands Are 'Ideal-Driven,'" MediaPost .com, January 2013, accessed October 28, 2013, http://www.mediapost .com/publications/article/165965/fastest-growing-brands-are-ideal-driven .html#axzz2j35EjnzF.

2. Reiman, Joey, "The Story of Purpose," accessed October 28, 2013, http://www .joeyreiman.com.

3. Sinek, Simon. "Start with Why," accessed October 28, 2013, http://www .startwithwhy.com.

4. Wells II, William R., "Semper Paratus: The Meaning," USCG.org, 2006, accessed October 28, 2013, http://www.uscg.mil/history/articles /SemperParatusTheMeaning.pdf.

## REFERENCES

5.  Jain, Sujata, "The Training It Takes to Become a Rescue Swimmer with the Coast Guard," Live5News.com, September 2013, accessed October 28, 2013, http://www.live5news.com/story/23395486/training-it-takes-to-become-a-rescueswimmer-with-the-us-coast-guard.

6.  Rasmus, Daniel W., "Defining Your Company's Vision," *Fast Company*, February 28, 2012. Accessed November 20, 2013, http://www.fastcompany.com/1821021/defining-your-companys-vision.

7.  "Richard Branson: The PT Barnum of British Business," Entrepreneur.com, October 2008, accessed October 28, 2013, http://www.entrepreneur.com/article/197616.

8.  Martin, Andrew, "Procter on Purpose," HubMagazine.com, *New York Times*, December 2010, accessed October 28, 2013, http://www.hubmagazine.com/html/2011/hub_42/may_jun/2372305742/procter-gamble_marc-pritchard.

9.  "Simon Sinek: How Great Leaders Inspire Action," Ted.com, September 2009, accessed October 28, 2013, http://www.ted.com/talks/simon_sinek_how_great_leaders_inspire_action.html.

## 06  WALK THE WALK

1.  UrbanDaddy.com, accessed October 29, 2013, http://www.urbandaddy.com/about.

2.  Meek, James, "It's a Gas," Guardian.co.uk, June 2001, accessed October 29, 2013, http://www.theguardian.com/lifeandstyle/2001/jun/28/healthandwellbeing.health.

3.  Schulz, Cory, "Statistics and Facts on the Cosmetics Industry," Statista.com, accessed October 29, 2013, http://www.statista.com/topics/1008/cosmeticsindustry/#chapter1.

4.  Frankel, Susannah, "Vivienne Westwood: 'You Have a More Interesting Life if You Wear Impressive Clothes,'" Independent.co.uk, September 2012, accessed October 29, 2013, http://www.independent.co.uk/news/people/profiles/vivienne-westwood-you-have-a-more-interesting-life-if-you-wear-impressiveclothes-8157187.html.

## 07 INSIGHT INTO DESIRE

1. Dao, James, and Thom Shanker, "No Longer a Soldier, Shinseki Has a New Mission," NYTimes.com, November 2009, accessed October 29, 2013, http://www.nytimes.com/2009/11/11/us/politics/11vets.html?pagewanted=all.

2. Mackay, Hugh, "What Makes Us Tick? The Ten Desires that Drive Us," CSU.edu.au, November 2010, accessed October 29, 2013, http://www.csu.edu.au/__data/assets/pdf_file/0011/118784/Hugh-McKay-speech.pdf.

3. Praetorious, Dean, "Coca-Cola Recipes to Celebrate 125 Years of Coke," HuffingtonPost.com, May 2011, accessed October 29, 2013, http://www.huffingtonpost.com/2011/05/08/coca-cola-recipes-125-years_n_859090.html#s275923title=Smoked_Ham_With.

4. Mackay, Hugh, "The 'Unfocused' Group Discussion Technique," RO.UOW.edu.au, accessed October 29, 2013, http://ro.uow.edu.au/buspapers/14/.

5. "SapientNitro's 'The Best Job in the World' Campaign Caps an Unprecedented. Awards Run with Best in Show and Four Gold Awards at MIXX," Sapient.com, October 2009, accessed October 29, 2013, http://www.sapient.com/en-us/news/press-releases/a1294.html.

## 08 IN THEIR SHOES

1. Edited by Paul Atkinson, Sara Delamont, Amanda Coffey, John Lofland, Lyn Lofland, "Ethography after Postmodernism," *Handbook of Ethnography*, London, Sage Publications. 2007: 445.

2. Bajarin, Tim, "A Smarter Future, Thanks to Sensors," *PC Magazine*, February 2013, accessed October 2013, http://www.pcmag.com/article2/0,2817,2415002,00.asp.

## 09 THE ORGANIZING IDEA

1. Lobo, Rita, "Marketing with Wings: Dietrich Mateschitz and the Art of Branding," EUROPEANCEO, October 16, 2013, accessed October 28, 2013,

http://www.europeanceo.com/home/featured/2013/10/marketing-with-wings -dietrich-mateschitz-and-the-art-of-branding.

2. Iezzi, Teressa, "Most Innovative Companies 2012: 29_Red Bull Media House," *Fast Company,* February 2012, accessed October 2013, http://www .fastcompany.com/3017413/most-innovative-companies-2012/29red-bull -media-house.

3. Bhatnagar, Parija, "Coke Slaps on a New Tagline," money.cnn.com, December 8, 2005, http://money.cnn.com/2005/12/08/news/fortune500/coke_meeting.

4. Shayon, Sheila, "Coca-Cola Continues to Open Happiness, from Coke Machine to Truck to Table," BrandChannel.com, September 2012, accessed October 30, 2013, http://www.brandchannel.com/home/post/2012/09/19 /Coca-Cola-Open-Happiness-091912.aspx.

5. "Coca-Cola NYSE-KO," Valueline.com, accessed October 30, 2013, http:// www3.valueline.com/dow30/f2084.pdf.

**11   WORLDS THAT SELL**

1. Cendrowski, Scott, "Nike's New Marketing Mojo," *CNN Money,* February 13, 2012, accessed October 2013, http://management.fortune.cnn .com/2012/02/13/nike-digital-marketing.

2. Hare, Emily, "Information Is Power; Stefan Olander," ContagiousMagazine .com, accessed October 30, 2013, http://www.contagiousmagazine.com/assets /magpdf/issue32/Interview_Olander_32.pdf.

3. Cendrowski, Scott, "Nike's New Marketing Mojo," *CNN Money,* February 13, 2012, accessed October 2013, http://management.fortune.cnn .com/2012/02/13/nike-digital-marketing.

4. Hare, Emily, "Information Is Power; Stefan Olander," ContagiousMagazine .com, accessed October 30, 2013, pp. 24/25, http://www.contagiousmagazine .com/assets/magpdf/issue32/Interview_Olander_32.pdf.

5.  Lynch, Kevin, "Good City Form," MITPress.mit.edu, February 1984, accessed October 31, 2013, http://mitpress.mit.edu/books/good-city-form.

## 12  SHOCK YOUR CULTURE

1.  Vella, Raphael. "Contemporary Art in Dialogue with . . . Politics and Education: Joseph Beuys as Teacher and Social Sculpture." Public Lecture Series for Malta Contemporary Art. Funded by Malta Arts Fund. March 2011. http://www.raphaelvella.com/Joseph-Beuys-as-Teacher-and-Social-Sculptor.pdf.

2.  Salter, Chuck, "Failure Doesn't Suck," *Fast Company,* May 2007. http://www.fastcompany.com/59549/failure-doesnt-suck.

3.  George, Shannon, "25 Memorable Doctor Seuss Quotes," Quotery.com, May 2013, accessed October 31, 2013, http://www.quotery.com/25-memorable-dr-seussquotes/.

4.  Spinelli, Mike, "How Carroll Shelby and a Gang of Nerds Beat Enzo Ferrari," May 2012, accessed October 31, 2013, http://jalopnik.com/5910453/how-carroll-shelby-and-a-gang-of-nerds-beat-enzo-ferrari.

# INDEX

# INDEX